BRIGHT IDEAS

A Green

CW00727785

Written by Colin Harris

Published by Scholastic Publications Ltd,
Marlborough House, Holly Walk,
Leamington Spa, Warwickshire CV32 4LS

Written by Colin Harris
Edited by Christine Lee
Sub-edited by Jackie Cunningham-Craig
Illustrated by Fred Haycock

Printed in Great Britain by Loxley Brothers Ltd,
Sheffield
© 1991 Scholastic Publications Ltd

Front and back covers designed by Sue Limb
Photograph by Martyn Chillmaid

British Library Cataloguing in Publication Data
Harris, Colin
    Bright ideas: a green school.
    1. Natural resources. Conservation
    I. Title
    333.7207

    ISBN 0-590-76505-1

Contents

Introduction

Green issues are everywhere; they are fashionable. Most daily newspapers have an environmental correspondent and some of the quality press have separate environmental sections. In this respect, green issues may be fashionable, but unlike fashion, they are highly unlikely to go away. They are part of our permanent agenda. In the autumn of 1990 the British government published its 'Green Bill' as a culmination of feverish debates over pollution, water quality, global warming, and other major concerns. Environmental interest is now a priority item, even on the international political agenda.

Key issues which now fill expert reports indicate a permanent preoccupation with the destruction of the rainforests, depletion of the ozone layer, and the atmospheric warming on a global scale, all pointing to a close and growing link between economic development and the environment.

Green issues, therefore, are to be perceived initially on a global level with major initiatives required by governments and international organisations. However, individuals can become effectively involved in local, but by no means less significant, processes. Waste management, loss of habitats, destruction of peatlands, planning permission for mineral workings, motorways and airports are all causes for local concern. If, therefore, we reasonably assume that concern with green issues is not going to go away, we need sustained and increased commitment to the kinds of action intended to ensure that there is a future on this planet for generations to come. Even young people appreciate this point.

Concern for the environment is not just a question of keeping things tidy. Litter has an obviously high profile rating because its effects are superficially obvious, but it is only a very small part of a highly complex waste management industry. We need to view it in perspective. Young people can hardly be held responsible for the state of the world environment; nevertheless, there

are adults who believe that anti-litter education is the principal means of environmental improvement.

Two main reasons will guarantee that green issues continue to be placed at the top of the agenda. Firstly, it is now recognised at the highest international levels that the environment is important; and secondly, governments now accept that conservation of natural environmental resources cannot be separated from economic policy for growth.

Business and local authorities share this concern and draft environmental clauses into their corporate and administrative plans. Individuals take up the challenge with demands for environmentally friendly goods and in pressing for accessible recycling facilities like bottle banks.

What are green issues? Until the last years of the 1980s, to be 'green' or 'environmental' was at best eccentric and at worst unhinged. Vegetarianism, open-toed sandals, marching with CND, were all parts of the syndrome. Now it is perfectly respectable to be concerned at the loss of wetlands or with the state of holiday beaches. However, with respectability has come responsibility, not just for our immediate surroundings with litter and frogspawn, but with global issues such as global warming caused by human activity and ozone-layer depletion.

The role of teachers in the environmental debate is consequently central. Environmental education can never be far from political education but the exertion of undue pressure is no part of a teacher's activity. Teaching by slogan (eg 'save the tropical forest'; 'save the whale') can highlight the superficial solutions without offering an appropriate level of understanding. We want to raise awareness and provide understanding that will enable children to make an educated response beyond the purely emotional one. Furthermore, can we really confront our pupils with a world apparently filled with unmitigated disasters? We cannot expect them to cope emotionally and intellectually with famine, starvation, the spread of deserts, the destruction of the rainforests, rising sea levels, water shortages, radio-active fallout, lack of oxygen, filthy beaches, dying dolphins and disappearing pandas, which could well be their learning diet if some of the admittedly important current environmental issues are allowed in their starkest forms on to the curriculum. The balance between making children aware and the need to prevent fear and panic becomes a major concern.

At the core of the question is how overt green issues should be within the total operation of a school. Ethical considerations determine the extent to which pupils become crusade fodder for the committed teacher, or are considered innocents who need to be protected from the hostile world.

This book aims to provide a range of practical suggestions for incorporating a concern for the environment into all appropriate operations of the school as a community of people with some kind of corporate loyalty and identity. Each suggestion relates to the broad curricular experience of pupils with clear implications for the hidden curriculum. Where appropriate, links with Attainment Targets of National Curriculum core and foundation subjects will be identified, in addition to cross-curricular themes. Obviously environmental education will be firmly supported in virtually all the activities.

Teachers seeking to use these ideas need to be sure of their own personal identification with the environmental cause. It would be counter-productive if practice were to be encouraged in pupils while not followed to a reasonable degree by the teachers.

Likewise, the school will need a whole institutional commitment to what is proposed, not as a sworn oath of allegiance to a green earth, but as a sensible model for pupils to follow. Just as societies throughout the world need to agree a firm environmental strategy, backed up by legislation where necessary, so schools need to build into their structures and practices a firm commitment to set an example.

GREEN SCHOOLS
The words, 'ecology', 'environmental', 'green', 'conservation' etc have now acquired a respectability, perhaps beyond the level at which they are understood. Ozone-friendly, for example, suggests the product is benign towards ozone, but at ground level ozone is harmful and contributes to serious air pollution. Similarly, 'ecological' is seen to be a positive attribute to a movement, a soap-powder, or to a resource centre.

Ecology is a science enabling students to understand the inter-dependence of living communities, both plants and animals, and their habitats. An ecological approach should form the principles which underlie a sound environmental education and which should inform all activities appropriate to a green school. Pupils should not be encouraged into activities which they cannot understand, even though there are progressive levels of understanding matching their abilities within which

appropriate environmental behaviour can be set. For example, there is no need for pupils to be aware of the relative economic costs of recycling paper and using pure new woodpulp before involving them in paper collection for recycling, but they do need to realise that not all paper is suitable for recycling and in consequence, they should not bring vast mixed bundles of paper and card and expect to save trees!

If the governors, staff and pupils of a school seek to implement the green suggestions described in this book, a base will be provided on which can be built a balanced and positive view of the environmental crisis. It should also be a happy and enjoyable experience for the pupils and will have the added advantage of involving parents.

SCHOOL GROUNDS
Major national initiatives have encouraged the use of school grounds for conservation and education, including grants from the Nature Conservancy Council and the Learning Through Landscapes Trust. Most local education authorities also offer advice. A school estate 'green audit' sets a pattern.

Specific reference is made to school grounds within the science, technology and geography National Curriculum requirements. Some schools have the clear advantage of existing natural habitats and potential wild areas, while others, especially those in urban areas, lack such opportunities. For this reason, suggestions for both urban and rural schools are included. Schools may use their grounds as a showcase to publicise their involvement with environmental issues.

SCHOOL BUILDINGS
While grounds represent the shop windows, school buildings are the 'shop floor', the working environment in which pupils and teachers spend most of their active time. From outside appearance to internal arrangement, from space for working to space for plants and animals, from colour and attractiveness to energy efficiency,

scope again exists for science and technology, as well as a context for other curricular subjects and cross-curricular issues.

MATERIALS
Much attention is paid to the use we make of resources. Schools can be involved in this through a review of materials used during lessons, for the maintenance of grounds and buildings, and in the dining room. Some aspects, such as purchasing policies, are beyond the competence of pupils but local authority staff dealing with supplies acquisition are often actively interested in materials that are environment-friendly. They welcome reciprocal interest from schools.

WASTE, RECYCLING AND POLLUTION
These are the high profile national concerns. We need to involve the whole school with suitable activities for all age groups, backed up with explanations of the ways in which waste and recycling can be managed. Much misinformation is circulating over waste, litter and recycling.

School policies on these should be linked with the development of responsible and caring attitudes.

Pollution studies, both within the school and beyond, can draw together conservation and education.

CAMPAIGNING
The final section draws the school into the local, national, and international communities through fund-raising, political action, and contact with conservation organisations.

MAIN SECTIONS
Each chapter consists of a short introduction outlining the main issues which form the background of the activities. Suggestions have been made in each case for both age range and group size. Your own knowledge and experience will determine the extent to which you stick to these limits as they are only an indication.

Under 'What you need' are listed some of the resources required for the successful completion of the activities. It is assumed in all cases, even if items are not listed, that

8

schools have reasonable access to paper, pencils, paints, adhesives, scissors etc and that a reasonable amount of horizontal and vertical display space is available.

'What to do' indicates first of all some of the background and purpose of the activity. Where appropriate, references may be made to cross-curricular links, to previous knowledge you may find it necessary for pupils to have, and a number of lead-in questions to raise pupils' awareness.

The National Curriculum occupies an increasing amount of primary teachers' time so apparently peripheral interest in green issues may cause a distraction from the main purpose of education. To counter this view, it can be argued that a green school offers an admirable and relevant context in which pupils can learn what is required from the National Curriculum and that the environment provides rich material for all areas of experience. The early subjects in the field – science, maths, English and technology – are given special mention but scope can be found for geography, history, music, art and PE.

WAYS OF TEACHING AND LEARNING
Teaching and learning experiences for pupils need to be seen as part of a green school approach. Three particular processes can be emphasised:
- enquiry-based learning;
- investigation;
- pupil-centred achievement.

ENQUIRY-BASED LEARNING
The initial stage of enquiry is the identification of an issue/theme/problem. Pupils become involved as active participants in a sequence of learning which includes opportunities for the development of skills. You can provide links between work done in the field and in the classroom. Open-ended enquiry, in which pupils are offered a range of stimuli related to environmental issues, helps in the clarification of attitudes and values.

For example, a consideration of recycling and use of materials will enable pupils to appreciate that resources need to be conserved and that in turn may affect their attitude to waste. Enquiry, above all, promotes learning that is cross-curricular. Issues concerning school buildings or the neighbourhood which may begin with a focus on, for example, the siting of a pedestrian crossing, will engage pupils in a range of investigations drawing on maths, English, geography, social education etc.

Some enquiry can be more teacher-directed, for example, weather study. But even here, channels of learning may spread out in all directions from the initial investigation.

INVESTIGATION
Investigation features prominently in enquiry learning and is integral to it. A series of investigations prompted by you can initiate enquiry. In some of the activities which follow, specific investigations are suggested as starting points. You will be able to identify similar approaches to most, if not all, activities. Questions like 'why is this?', 'what do you see?', 'can you explain?' and 'what if . . .?' will lead into investigations.

PUPIL-CENTRED ACHIEVEMENT

Pupil-centred achievement is fundamental to a successful green school. It is not enough for you to initiate and carry through a whole series of quite laudable projects if they do not involve pupils in active participation and satisfying achievement. This is not to say that a green school is at all smug; a balanced appraisal of success or failure are all part of the learning process.

Schools, therefore, need to identify aspects of the activities which will give pupils a sense of ownership and achievement. Involving them in all stages of an activity's development is an obvious way forward, as is the display of work recognising class and individual contributions. While arrangements for assessment within the National Curriculum are only now being clarified, schools have an obligation to devise assessment policies for core and foundation subjects, and later guidelines will help them to measure achievement in cross-curricular themes like environmental education.

PLANNING FOR A GREEN SCHOOL

You could, if you choose, dip into this book for a number of practical suggestions which might help when inspiration is lacking. This, however, would be a disservice to pupils. If the purpose behind the book is to be achieved, forward planning is essential. Activities such as recycling paper and conserving energy would be to little purpose if they were taken up for a week or two and then dropped.

On the other hand, there is clearly a danger of overkill if every single activity of the school is explicitly linked to a green policy. Pupils and parents would lose interest and ask for a more balanced approach.

Some activities involving, for example, mounting a display or visiting a nature reserve, have immediate impact and could be sources of inspiration. Some courses of action requiring the making of bird boxes or wind vanes may lead to later applications, for example during nesting time or when weather recordings are being made. The setting up of a wild flower garden is a much longer term project which will only come to fruition after a year or two. Pupils should be discouraged from expecting instant success with fragrant butterfly-attracting plants springing up overnight!

This means you carefully thinking through a programme of activities with flexibility to respond to topical issues and pupils' enthusiasms, and taking into account the need for all members of the school community to play their parts.

Above all, a school's green programme must be realistic in terms of both physical and human resources. Pupils must not be allowed to develop inflated expectations of what they and the staff can achieve, so their goals must be attainable. Only set out to implement schemes that are perceived to be important by pupils and staff. Inevitably some projects will not succeed as expected. It is a good experience for pupils to contend with failure, even if it can be frustrating when vandals keep throwing things into the pond. They must learn to face reality, while you need to explain why failure has occurred. Next time success might be possible.

One way forward would be to take a limited number of activities from each section and as a staff decide which ones you will attempt. Those relating to school grounds will be heavily dependent on the richness of the existing environment. Some schools, with particularly attractive buildings, may decide to emphasise the

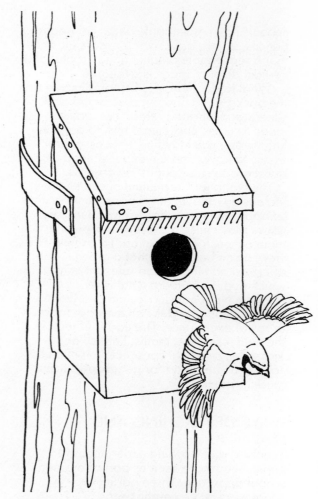

working environment of classrooms, hall etc. Local circumstances may also restrict recycling activities, so emphasis may be better placed on use of materials or campaigning.

In all cases you should seek a balance between the short term inspirational activities, those that lead to action, and the long-term projects in which goals are achieved in years rather than months.

No school will be able to attempt all the activities suggested in this book. They represent a sample of suggestions designed to encourage a more environmentally-aware school population.

Two outcomes are possible. The first relates to the environment. Most activities are designed not just to raise awareness but to encourage active participation in conservation, both of wildlife and of resources.

The second concerns the curriculum. The National Curriculum Council document Curriculum Guidance 7: Environmental Education, offers advice to schools on the implementation of environmental education as a cross-curricular theme within the National Curriculum. While this theme should not be seen in isolation, and links with the others on careers, health education, economic and industrial understanding and citizenship, it does find a place in the primary school through the knowledge and understanding required for core and foundation subjects. For many it represents an integrating structure for topic work.

You will find the knowledge, skills and attitudes listed in CG7 raise a host of issues covered by the activities in this book. Likewise, all schools will have received a copy of This Common Inheritance: A Survey of the White Paper on the Environment, which, while it seeks to explain government policy on environmental issues, does indicate courses of action for all. It further links the curriculum to the use of school grounds in support of environmental education. These two books stamp official approval on ideas for green schools.

STRUCTURE
You are guided to consider environmental education in a structure comprising three linked components:
- Education *about* the environment (knowledge and understanding);
- Education *for* the environment (values, attitudes and actions);
- Education *in* or *through* the environment (skills, using the environment as a resource). This is not an original concept but it may be particularly helpful to those whose personal commitment to conservation prompts them to incorporate environmental concerns into their schemes of work or topic plans. Each

activity in this book links with at least one of these components, with the particular intention of encouraging action *for* the environment. All suggestions can be linked with specific attainment targets within the National Curriculum.

POLICY
The selection of one or more of the suggested activities will achieve little if taken in isolation. It is necessary to review all these ideas in the context of whole school policies. Reference is made in appropriate activities to the advantage of a whole school approach, with campaigning, for example, in which all staff and pupils can be involved.

Consistent with an agreed course of action is an environmental education policy forming an important segment of the school's general curriculum statement. Within the terms of the ERA, schools are required to adopt a policy for curriculum and CG7 argues for environmental education being integral to that policy. It follows, therefore, that a member of staff needs to assume responsibility for co-ordinating both green school activities and an environmental education policy within which these activities can be given curricular relevance.

Some schools may need help in drafting policy statements. LEA advisers may be available to assist, but further guidance and suggestions can be obtained from The Council for Environmental Education (see Resources, page 124).

Finally, schools are not going to save the world on their own by adopting green approaches to curriculum and action, but we can provide our pupils with hopeful and positive ways forward to counterbalance some of the more negative messages they may be hearing.

School grounds

Attention is now being focussed on school grounds to supplement fieldwork in other localities in support of the National Curriculum. The Learning Through Landscapes Trust (see Resources, page 124) together with *The Outside Classroom* (DES) indicate in some detail both the scope for school grounds for conservation and education and technical requirements for developing their use. Ideally, an overall plan for school grounds should be considered but it is possible to undertake one or two activities if major developments are out of the question.

Whatever the status of the school under LMS, it only functions as a tenant of the land and any substantial change to the landscape must only be undertaken with prior permission of the authority. In most cases care of school grounds will be in the hands of contractors who will need to have conservation criteria built into their grounds specification and be involved in any schemes to establish nature reserves or plant trees. Some schools have discovered wild flowers mown and log piles flattened when work has been done without informing grounds staff. Similar arrangements will be necessary if you try to establish a vegetable plot. Playing fields should not be ploughed up for this purpose without consulting grounds maintenance staff!

School grounds feature prominently in a number of National Curriculum attainment targets. They include:
Science 1: Exploration of science
Science 2: The variety of life
Science 5: Human influences on the earth
Science 9: Earth and atmosphere
Science 11: Sound and music
Science 16: The earth in space
Mathematics 9: Using and applying mathematics
Mathematics 12: Handling data (Collect, record and process data)
Mathematics 13: Handling data (Represent and interpret data)
English 1: Speaking and listening
English 2: Reading
English 3: Writing
Technology 1: Identifying needs and opportunities
Technology 2: Generating a design
Technology 3: Planning and making
Proposals for geography assume the school grounds will be used as the basis for a variety of geographical explorations including some incorporated in science:
Geography 1: Geographical skills
Geography 3: Physical geography
Geography 5: Environmental geography
Specific reference is made to school grounds in environmental education cross-curricular guidance.

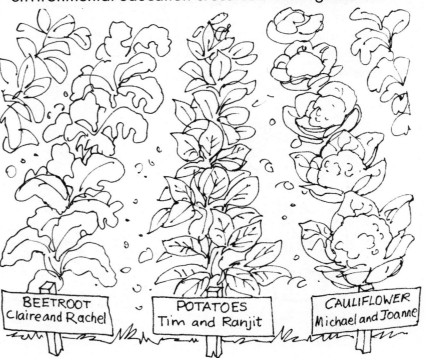

BEETROOT Claire and Rachel   POTATOES Tim and Ranjit   CAULIFLOWER Michael and Joanne

A green audit

Age range
Seven to eleven.

Group size
Whole class, working in pairs.

What you need
Clipboards and pencils, sketch pads, maps of school site, polaroid camera (optional).

What to do
The purpose of this activity is to develop pupils' observation skills as part of an assessment of the school grounds for promoting environmental understanding. The audit is designed to allow pupils freedom to note what they find particularly interesting and attractive in the school grounds. The results are not as important as the process.

Ask the children to work in pairs to discover, in broad terms, what the school grounds contain in the way of attractive features like trees, flower beds and play apparatus, as well as less attractive features like blank walls and untidy corners. Explain that this is an attempt to assess the general appearance of the site:
- As visitors might see it as they arrive;
- As pupils see it.

Encourage them to make notes and quick sketches of any interesting features, and to use the map to record what they observe.

Other aspects that could be noted, where appropriate, include the amount of litter, signs of wildlife, opportunities for play etc.

Ask each pair to draw up and agree a list of five key words which describe for them the atmosphere of the school grounds. For example, 'dusty', 'green', 'exciting', might be some they could choose.

Follow-up
● The key word exercise could lead into a whole class discussion of the atmosphere of the site, with an agreed list of words most commonly chosen.
● Features recorded on individual maps could be incorporated on to a large map for wall display in the classroom.
● The sketches can be displayed around the map with a key to their location. It is important for pupils to appreciate the difference between a map and a sketch.
● Findings can be used as a preliminary survey for siting a nature reserve.
● Suggestions could be drawn up for improvements to the site, placing of litter bins, notice-boards, planting schemes etc.

Drawing a map

Age range
Five to eleven.

Group size
Individuals or whole class, depending on the approach selected.

What you need
For younger pupils: base board on which to 'build' a map, Lego or other suitable three-dimensional materials, boxes, scissors, adhesive, fabric and other craft materials. For older pupils; a compass, large blank sheets of paper, pencils and coloured crayons.

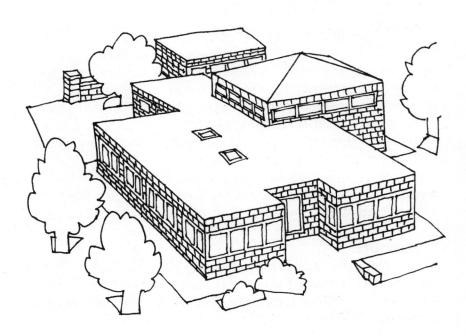

What to do

Maps are fundamental to geographical understanding. This activity gives an opportunity to develop early map skills based on observations of the school estate. Concepts of direction, scale and representational key can be introduced to older pupils, with younger ones using a more simplified approach.

Explain to younger pupils that the board is like the school grounds. Ask them to describe what there is in the grounds and use Lego or other materials to represent these features. They can say where each item should go. This will help them understand scale.

Ask older pupils to use a compass to align the large sheets of paper, and then in groups observe and draw the position of identified features of the school grounds. It may be necessary for them to walk around the grounds to find out where important features are. They should include gates, paths, playgrounds, outlines of buildings, trees and apparatus. A scale can be included if rough dimensions can be paced.

An alternative to both suggestions would be for the pupils to imagine they were in a balloon above the school and to draw what they can see.

Follow-up

Maps can be displayed on the wall and features added during the course of further green activities. For example, wild areas, ponds etc can be indicated as and when they are developed.

Planning a wildlife area

Age range
Five to eleven.

Group size
Whole class working individually or in small groups.

What you need
A suitable area of the school grounds, paper and pencils, measuring tape, marker pegs, string, a selection of books on wildlife areas.

What to do
This activity can be undertaken even if you do not intend to carry the plan through to fruition. If you do plan to implement it then careful arrangements should be made with the appropriate grounds maintenance authorities. The selection of site should be made in advance by the teacher. This will require the full co-operation of all staff, but particularly of the headteacher. Local provision for advice and assistance might be available.

It is important to find out well beforehand.

Select a suitable area of the school grounds, preferably a corner with a boundary hedge or other natural feature. Prepare for the pupils a simple sketch map, indicating the extent of the wild area by means of marker pegs in the ground. Let a small group of children measure the area and mark the distances on the map.

Introduce the idea of a wild area/nature reserve by asking the pupils if they know what it is and what it is for. Why do we 'create' such areas? Discuss with the children the value of these areas to wildlife and the value to themselves in the development of their appreciation of the environment.

Let the class work individually, or in small groups, and either copy the map or work from a photocopy and make their own design. Items for the wildlife area could include a pond, bird-table, wild flower plots, meadow, planted area of trees and shrubs, wet area, log piles, bird boxes etc.

Let the children discuss each other's plans. Can they explain why they have chosen to include particular items?

Follow-up
● Select the best features of all suggested plans and attempt to implement them.
● Draw up a time-table for implementation.
● Discuss who is going to do the work and how money can be raised.
● If a real wild area cannot be created, pupils should make a model to include all the features you agreed with them.
● Pupils can write a short piece on why they think wild areas are a good idea.

Urban ideas
Wildlife interest can be established in an urban setting by using bird tables, small ponds and plants in tubs or other large containers.

Moving around

Age range
Seven to eleven.

Group size
Whole class working in pairs.

What you need
Silva compasses, maps of school grounds, clipboards and pencils.

What to do
A simple treasure trail can lead to interesting discoveries. Pupils will need guidance if they are to produce a satisfactory trail, so you may wish to predetermine the features which will provide focal points on the trail.

Ask the children to work in pairs and make their own compass trails around the school grounds, using either four or eight points of the compass to determine direction. Ask them to start from a fixed point in the school grounds then move in a given direction to a feature of interest, pacing the distance then writing a question about the feature. For example, the trail might read 'Move SE for ten paces: what do you see on your right?' and so on. Ask the children to make sure that their compass trails always end back where they started.

Let the children try out each other's trails and write notes on what they find at the various points. The whole activity can be related to number work and language development. For example, children can be asked to count the number of logs in a pile, or write a description of a flower bed.

It is important to emphasise the environmental

relevance of this activity which helps pupils to appreciate the richness of their surroundings.

Creating habitats

Age range
Five to eleven.

Group size
Small group to whole class.

What you need
Pond liner, paving stones, aquatic plants, marsh plants, chalk, wild flower seeds, selected shrubs, logs, corrugated metal sheet. Contact your local garden centre or environmental education adviser for guidance on where to buy more expensive items and on possible grant aid.

What to do

A selection of easily created habitats is suggested here, some of which can be set up in a very short time, while others require forward planning for up to a year. The point at which you introduce the idea to pupils will depend on the required degree of preparation. Most can be developed from earlier activities such as planning a wildlife area. In some cases (indicated with an asterisk) more detailed research should be undertaken and suggestions for further reading are given on page 127. Only brief guidance is given here.

The purpose behind these habitats is essentially to attract or introduce wildlife to the school grounds. Involve the pupils in discussing what you plan to do and why you are doing it.

Each separate habitat provides a rich resource for ecological investigations. The concept of habitats interacting with living things is fundamental to the whole 'green' approach. Interdependence can be appreciated when a small scale example is available for study.

Pond*

This requires forward planning and a site needs to be chosen away from trees and potential vandalism.

Dig a hole a minimum of one metre deep, with at least one side gently shelving, and line it with suitable material (butyl or clay are best). If sheet liner is used, anchor it with paving stones and form a hard standing edge to the pond. Fill it with water and leave it for several days before installing oxygenating, marginal and other plants (see Figure 1).

A pond is one of the most satisfying habitats to create, but expect some problems, especially if you have a thin liner that could be easily punctured. Safety aspects

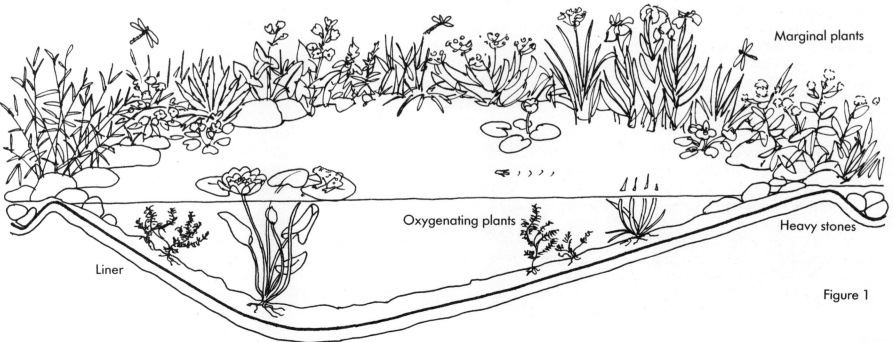

Marginal plants

Oxygenating plants

Liner

Heavy stones

Figure 1

should also be considered, which is why the edges should be made shallow.

Stocking the pond requires specialised local advice. Contact a garden centre or local wildlife trust.

Wet area
A wet area can offer a more exciting range of plants and animal life than ponds. Dig a shallow hole approximately 0.5 metre deep, line it with black sheeting plastic, and infill it with suitable soil. Plant marsh-loving species. Contact a garden centre for suitable species.

Chalk mound
This is only possible in certain parts of the country where chalk is available from roadwork excavations etc. Sow or plant chalkland flora as a contrast to flora found on other soil types of the local area.

Wild flower meadow
It is worth leaving a patch of grass to grow uncut, if only to discover species suppressed by mowing. Pupils can monitor and identify plants as they grow. Grass will need to be mown once or twice a year depending on the flowers you wish to encourage.

Alternatively, clear an area and sow wild flower seeds mixed with grass seed to create a tailor-made meadow. Expert advice should be sought on the selection of seed varieties. The Nature Conservancy Council issues helpful leaflets.

Wild flower books and the use of identification keys provide curriculum opportunities for pupils.

Butterfly garden*
This needs to be part of the wild flower meadow as well as the main wildlife area plan. Certain shrub species can be chosen for their insect attracting properties. These include hemp agrimony, buddleia, michaelmas daises and heliotropum. Nettles and other wild plants can also be incorporated. Full lists are included in several books on the reference list (see page 127).

Pupils should be warned not to expect an invasion of butterflies as soon as the shrubs are planted. Careful monitoring will reveal how short the season is for certain butterfly species.

Log piles
This is an interesting activity which can involve even the youngest child. Place logs for pupils to use as seats

around the school grounds. After a few weeks show the children how the undersides quickly become havens for invertebrate life. A pile of larger logs in the corner of the wildlife area can be left for frogs, hedgehogs and more invertebrates.

Follow-up
When the habitats have been created they need to be systematically observed and monitored. With the pupils, draw up an observation rota appropriate to each habitat:
- Quadrats can be used to draw up species lists in flower meadows;
- Records can be kept on a monthly basis and changes noted;
- The established pond can be used for dipping and pupils encouraged to identify species;
- Butterfly species visiting the wild area can be identified and recorded.
   Gradually the school will build up a set of interesting and important records.

Urban ideas
Most habitats suggested here can be adapted for urban schools. Enclosed and fully paved courtyards can accommodate a pond if some slabs are lifted and a preformed liner put in their place. Shrubs and wild flowers can easily be grown in pots and tubs. Charts on urban wildlife (see Resources, page 124) offer further suggestions.

Planting trees and hedges

Age range
Seven to eleven.

Group size
Whole class working in small groups.

What you need
Spades, small trees or saplings, guards, ties and stakes, black plastic sheeting, compost, hedging plants, copies of photocopiable pages 113 and 114.

What to do
This activity should take place during winter while trees are dormant.
   Ask the children the reasons for planting trees. Discuss any recent storms and whether any trees were uprooted. Some children may refer to the destruction of the rainforest. Ask the class to think of ways in which we are dependent upon trees. Pupils may have some interesting ideas, but they need to realise that people use trees for shelter, shade, colour, oxygen, wood etc. Trees need to be planted to replace those that die or are cut down.

Working closely with the headteacher and grounds maintenance staff, select suitable sites for tree planting and hedging, bearing in mind the size of trees when mature. The selection of suitable sites needs careful thought. Take into account depth of root affecting school foundations, shading out classrooms, leaf fall near ponds etc.

When choosing trees for planting, consult grounds maintenance staff, governors, and outside groups interested in providing advice and help, for example, landscape architects, Groundwork Trust, and local wildlife trusts. Use only native species. The Woodland Trust has some interesting materials for pupils, including a chart explaining the growth rate of trees.

If possible, allow one tree per pupil or a number of trees per class for reasons of ownership. Careful watering in the early stages of growth is essential so

care for plants is encouraged. Photocopiable page 113 gives advice on planting saplings, while page 114 provides a record chart.

Follow-up
Monitor closely the development of the planted area. Measure and record growth rates and relative sizes. Note early animal life as it is attracted to trees, especially insects and birds.

Urban ideas
Most school playgrounds will yield one or two places where suitable trees can be planted.

Species like horse chestnut can be grown in tubs until they are too big and will need to be transplanted to a park. Before growing your sapling, discuss its final location with your local council.

Attracting animals

Age range
Seven to eleven.

Group size
Whole class.

What you need
Wood for making bird and bat boxes, roofing felt, bird table, bird identification books.

What to do
The purpose of this activity is to involve pupils in practical construction work as part of their technology experience, and to encourage them to be involved in the care of living creatures. They need to appreciate that a

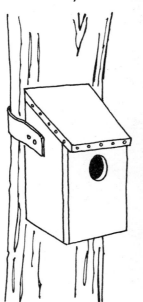

green school is prepared to provide for some of the needs of animals. Ask pupils to suggest ways of attracting animals. Discuss feeding, nesting and roosting.

Let the pupils help to design and make bird and bat boxes. Tit boxes are the most popular, but in suitable localities other species can be expected to nest in boxes of different designs. Bat boxes are equally important from a wildlife standpoint but are less useful for educational purposes as pupils are unlikely to be able to observe active animals.

Site boxes on north facing walls or high on the north side of trees. This provides shelter from the sun for young birds.

Set up bird tables so that they are inaccessible to cats, then fill them with wild bird food. The RSPB suggests suitable diets for a variety of birds. Care must be taken not to feed birds with hard foods such as peanuts during the nesting season, as nuts can choke newly-hatched birds. There is no need to provide extra food during the summer. Provide a dish of water for drinking and bathing and remind the children that it should be kept ice-free during the winter.

Follow-up
Keep careful records of the birds observed, both in the nesting boxes and on the feeding table. Use these observations to make a seasonal diary of bird visitors. When tits are nesting, pupils can note the frequency of trips from the nest to find food. What food do the parents bring? What is their behaviour when leaving and returning?

How many different species of birds visit the bird table in winter? Do different ones come on cold days? What diet does each bird prefer? Do some prefer to feed on the ground and not on the table?

Graphs and diagrams can be drawn using the data collected during these observations.

Display pictures of the more common species where the table can be observed without disturbing the birds.

Growing for green

Age range
Five to eleven.

Group size
Whole school, working in small groups on a rota basis.

What you need
Leaflets from supermarkets about organic produce, a selection of 'organic' and 'non-organic' vegetables, area to make a vegetable plot, full size garden tools for teachers, smaller tools for pupils, vegetable seeds or plants, organic fertiliser.

What to do
The purpose of this whole school activity is to grow a limited supply of 'organic' vegetables, produced without the aid of chemical sprays and artificial fertilisers.

Take to school a selection of supermarket leaflets explaining organically grown vegetables. Ask pupils what they think 'organically grown' means. Ask them why they think farmers use chemical sprays. Compare an 'organic' carrot with a clean straight one.

Let the children try to grow their own 'organic' vegetables. To achieve this, a small plot should be allocated to each class, who will be responsible for preparing the ground, planting/sowing, cultivating and weeding, and finally harvesting. Younger pupils may be unable to sustain an entire programme so infants may be linked with juniors to encourage co-operation.

Follow-up
Record-keeping is an important follow-up to this activity, with notes kept of planting dates, costs, frequency of watering, rates of growth etc to achieve useful comparisons. If enough produce is harvested, it can be sold to parents.

Urban ideas
Grow-bags or tubs could replace garden plots. Some could be grown indoors, especially tomatoes. Encourage the children to consider the implications of using peat-based grow-bags. Are there any viable alternatives? Organisations such as Friends of the Earth will be happy to advise.

The air around

Age range
Five to eleven.

Group size
Whole class working individually or in small groups.

What you need
Meteorological instruments (either commercially produced or improvised), copies of photocopiable pages 115 and 116.

What to do
The weather is an aspect of the environment which we constantly experience. Eventual understanding of such concepts as global warming, drought etc needs to be preceded by investigations of local weather phenomena.

Weather studies feature in National Curriculum requirements for both geography and science and frequently form a focus for topic work. As the weather is one of the commonest conversation topics, pupils will be familiar with the subject and can readily be introduced to this activity.

Ask the children to comment on the day's weather: hot, cold, wet, dry, windy, cloudy, etc. Let them keep a daily record of weather observations to include as many

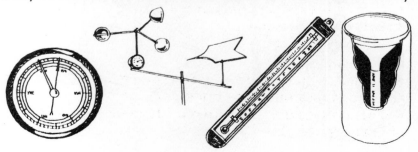

of the following conditions and instruments as are appropriate to the age group:
● Temperature – thermometer;
● Rainfall – rain gauge;
● Wind speed and direction – anemometer and weather vane;
● Cloud cover – chart;
● Atmospheric pressure – barometer;
● Relative humidity – wet/dry bulb thermometer.
Emphasise the need for accurate measurements to be made and the results recorded as part of a scientific study. Sample record charts are given on pages 115 and 116.

Let the children record temperatures at different points of the school grounds. It may be possible to detect a number of micro-climates and to discover why official temperatures are always taken in the shade. Use a variety of charts, both pictorial and statistical, to record observations.

Follow-up
Let the children use their charts to compare the weather conditions they observe with those they know of in different parts of the world. Encourage them to assess what wet, dry, hot and cold mean when we talk about the weather.

Coping with concrete

Age range
Five to eleven.

Group size
Whole school.

What you need
Breeze blocks, old tyres, paving stones, bird feeder, paint and brushes, tubs, window boxes, wild flower seeds, soil, gardening tools, plants, bulbs.

What to do
Many urban schools have no green areas or gardens, apart from a tree or two. Some are completely concreted. Encourage the children to plan activities to emphasise that your school has 'gone green' even if this is the case. This will mean going back to your 'green audit' and concentrating on all the positive aspects of the school.

Let the children try out some of the following ideas:
• Create small gardens using raised beds behind breeze blocks;
• Create sculptures from sturdy items like tyres and paving stones;
• Hang out a bird feeder;
• Paint bare walls with artistic murals;
• Group large tubs together in quiet corners and sow wild flower seeds in them;
• Construct window boxes if there are suitable ledges;
• Grow climbing plants like honeysuckle and clematis in large tubs and train them over unsightly sheds and fuel stores;
• Grow bulbs in a variety of containers;
• Paint the playground.

Follow-up
• Further schemes can be developed from ideas in *The Outdoor Classroom* (see page 127).
• Encourage pupils to take a pride in the appearance of their school.

School buildings

The built environment should always feature in any schemes for incorporating environmental education in the school curriculum. It is frequently neglected in favour of the natural world, but is no less a component of pupils' surroundings, especially in the case of urban schools.

Building types vary as much as school estates, so this chapter makes no assumptions about the age, condition or siting of your school. Activities will need to be chosen according to individual circumstances. The activities in this chapter are arranged in a particular order, beginning with the external appearance of the school, and then moving in and about the building, focussing first on general layout and then on the use of individual classrooms.

While the starting point for most activities is identifying and promoting positive attitudes to pupils' environments, the curriculum opportunities are many and varied. Design and technology is considered in architectural features, structure and materials which together make up the building and its component parts. Science is featured in a consideration of materials and in energy efficiency.

Mathematics is concerned with shape as well as number and English contributes spoken and written commentaries on all activities. Early map work using the building and classroom layout as a basis for scale, distance and direction develops geographical skills, and history can be accommodated if the school occupies an older building.

Specific attainment targets can be referred to as follows:
Science 1: Explanation of science
Science 6: Types and uses of materials
Science 13: Energy
Mathematics 1: Using and applying mathematics
Mathematics 4: Estimate and approximate in number
Mathematics 8: Estimate and measure quantities, and appreciate the approximate nature of measurement.
Mathematics 9: Use shape and space and handle data in practical tasks
Mathematics 10 & 11: Shape and space
Mathematics 12 & 13: Handling data
English 1: Speaking and listening
English 2: Reading
English 3: Writing
Technology 1: Identifying needs and opportunities
Technology 2: Generating and design
Technology 3: Planning and making
Technology 4: Evaluation
Geography 1: Geographical skills

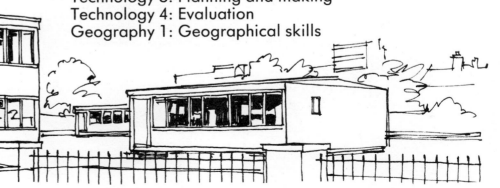

Outside in 1

Age range
Five to seven.

Group size
Whole class.

What you need
Cartons, shoe boxes, paint, sugar paper, adhesive.

What to do
The aim of this activity is to develop an awareness of spatial relationships. It will also help in the development of geographical concepts through observation. The children need no prior knowledge of maps and can be introduced to the activity through questions such as 'what does the school look like from outside?'. If they are unfamiliar with models you may need to show them one and explain 'It is like the real thing but smaller'!

Take the class into the playground and ask the children to look closely at the way in which the building is constructed. Discuss with pupils the various features, such as the hall, roof etc.

Back in the classroom, ask the children to make a model of the school buildings, using either large cartons piled on the floor, or smaller boxes on tables.

The model can be made more permanent by sticking the boxes together. Let the children paint their model in colours to match the real appearance and ask them to make finer details such as chimneys from sugar paper.

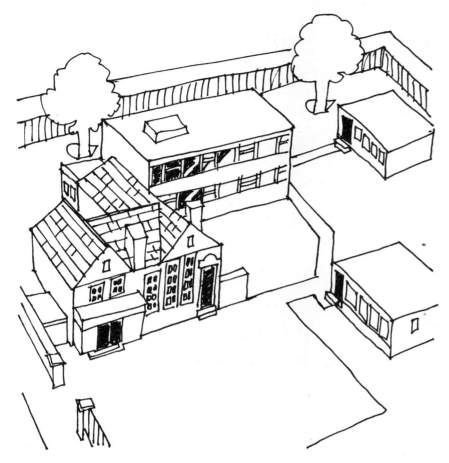

When the model is finished ask the pupils to say what they like about the real school building and also what they do not like about it. Make a list of the descriptive words the children use and display it alongside the model, labelled 'Our school . . .'.

Follow-up
The model represents what the school is like. A development would be to add improvements suggested by pupils in response to the question 'How can we make the school look better?'.

Outside in 2

Age range
Seven to eleven.

Group size
Whole class, working in groups of five or six.

What you need
Drawing and sugar paper, coloured paper, paint, tape measure, clinometer, scissors, adhesive.

What to do
The aim of this activity is to observe and record the external features of the school building, including windows, doors, building materials etc. Careful observation of a familiar feature like the school building will identify several details that pupils may not have previously noticed. Begin by asking them about one or two rather obscure features you have noticed to test their awareness. Suggest that outside appearances are important and ask the children to investigate what their school looks like and suggest how it can be improved.

Encourage the children to work in groups to make detailed drawings of features such as windows and doors, and to draw the elevation of each side of the building, either as a sketch or using the measuring tape to make a scale drawing. Height can be calculated using the clinometer.

Back in the classroom, ask the children to enlarge their 'field sketches' or drawings and cut them out as silhouettes from sugar or other coloured paper. Mount and display the silhouettes, indicating the direction of the elevation. The aim is to display a continuous profile/silhouette of the four sides of the school so they can all be seen at once.

Members of each group can add and label details such as drain pipes, flower beds, windows, doors, dustbins etc.

Follow-up
This work can be used as a starting point for a range of enquiries into architectural features, building structures and aesthetic aspects which could be linked to art and technology.

This should then develop into a consideration of what the building looks like to visitors, especially those who call at school for the first time. Pupils can then suggest ways in which its attractiveness can be enhanced. Perhaps the state of the paintwork will be noted and action recommended!

Urban ideas
Some urban schools may not have sufficient space for all elevations to be treated in this way, but the main approach could nevertheless be drawn and represented in the way indicated.

What is it made of?

Age range
Nine to eleven.

Group size
Whole class (including group and individual work).

What you need
A range of locally used building materials, labels, clipboards, pictures/drawings of buildings.

What to do
This activity will help pupils to identify a variety of materials in their immediate environment and consider the range of uses to which they are put. Initially, this will be very much a teacher-directed enquiry, but children will eventually be given opportunities for direct investigation when they study the external features of the building.

Arrange a display of building materials (include both local and non-local examples for variety) suitably labelled, for pupils to investigate and discuss in pairs. Ask them simple questions such as what is it made of? or, what is it used for? Include unexpected items like wire and plastic tubing, as well as the more obvious materials such as breeze blocks and timber.

Alternatively, materials can be passed around or arranged on numbered tables so that pupils can work in groups.

Next, let the class go outside with clipboards to survey the school building and note all the different materials used in its construction, indicating what they are all used for.

Follow-up
Discuss the purpose of building materials. They can be structural (ie to hold the building up), to protect (ie keep out wind, rain, cold and heat), to allow light in, to retain heat etc. Ask pupils to suggest how successful the building materials are in supporting their 'green' approach.

Further follow-up can include notes being added to a collection of pictures of buildings. A useful source of photographs is an estate agent where dozens of photographs may not be required after houses and other buildings are sold. Ask the children to identify and record the purpose of the various building materials, writing the details on mounting card around the picture.

Urban ideas
There is likely to be a wider range of types of buildings near urban schools, so this activity could be the start of an urban environment study.

First impressions

Age range
Five to eleven.

Group size
Whole school.

What you need
A variety of plant holders, low tables, wall hangings, pottery, chairs, materials for making welcome notices.

What to do
This activity has a twofold purpose. It will involve pupils in using art, craft and design work to create a pleasant area for visitors and it will enable them to display some of their curricular work. The displays can then be used as an aid to learning.

The school entrance must create the right impression when visitors enter. It should be obvious that this is a 'green' school. Basic furniture and carpet or rugs need to be provided, paying particular attention to materials. Natural fibres for the rug and no tropical hardwoods for the furniture are just two aspects which could be considered.

Arrange for each class to take responsibility for arranging displays in the entrance hall for a limited period, perhaps half a term, on a rota basis. The theme for displays can reflect a range of 'green concerns' and

also be linked to the curriculum and to other aspects of school life. For example, seasonal festivities, parent and governor interest, anniversaries, school journeys, field work, campaigns etc.

'Living' displays of plants, and to a lesser extent animals, can stem from other green initiatives such as growing plants, flowers and organic vegetables from seeds and cuttings. Animal displays should be restricted to those that have green approval, ie a small aquarium as an eco-system, but *not* captive wild animals!

If ideas are discussed beforehand by teachers so that up to a year ahead can be planned, the display can be linked to curricular work by guiding pupils to observe, make note of, and use later, certain aspects of the exhibits. For example, a collection of geological specimens might be on display for which observation of shape, size, colour, texture and composition can be carried out as part of geography and science work. Particularly attractive arrangements could feature as a stimulus to drawing and painting.

Moving about

Age range
Five to seven.

Group size
Five or six, up to whole class.

What you need
Small pieces of card, felt-tipped pens, Blu-Tack, stop-watch (optional).

What to do
The purpose of this activity is to consider routes people take when moving from one place to another. Can we do this without disturbing anyone? Map skills are developed through this activity, particularly regarding direction. Some maths skills are needed if time and distance are calculated.

Prepare two sets of card for each group. On each card write a room or known location within the school (eg Head's office, Mrs Dunn's room, dining hall etc). Shuffle the cards and let the children draw one in turn from each set. They then have to describe from memory

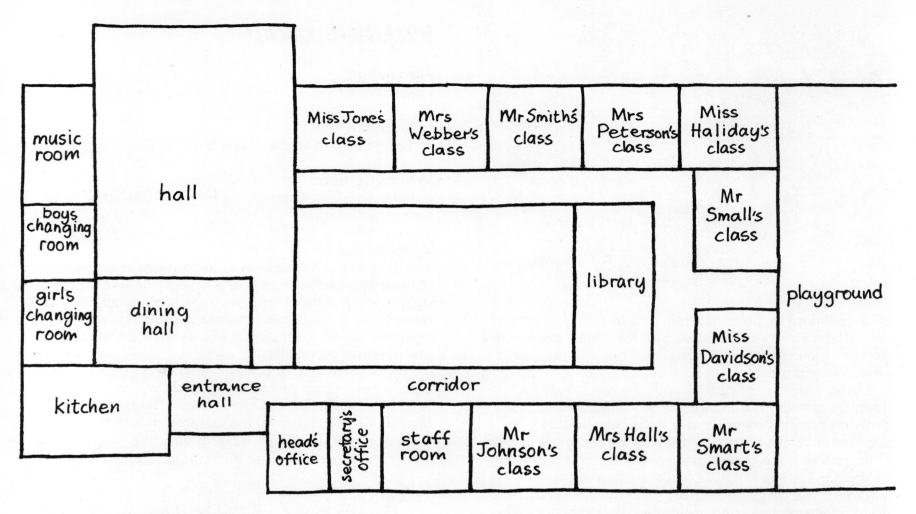

how they would get from one location to the other.

Encourage the use of direction words like left and right to describe their 'journey'. Once all the pairs are matched, pupils can describe what they would see as they go from one location to another and if possible find out how far each journey is and how long it takes to get from one location to another. At any point during the game the cards can be reshuffled to add extra journeys.

Some pupils engaging in this activity may be new to the school and it can be used to help them find their way around. With very young children who are unable to read the cards the help of an older pupil is desirable.

Prepare a simple map showing the layout of the school and allow older pupils to draw on the routes. You may discover that signs and directions need to be indicated at certain points in the school to help visitors.

Follow-up
Use any of the following ideas with older children:
- Get the children to form pairs and ask one child in each pair to describe a journey from an agreed starting point such as the entrance hall. Her partner then has to say what the destination is. This activity could alternatively be written rather than spoken. This involves geography skills.
- Ask the children to find out how long it takes to get from one part of the school to another, using the stop-watch and no faster pace than a walk, then show their findings in tables and graphs. This involves mathematics skills.
- Let the children undertake a survey of pupil movements during arrival, break, lunchtime and home-time. Where are there bottlenecks, traffic jams, empty spaces etc? What improvements can they suggest for more efficient movement? This activity involves geography and technology.
- Ask the children to write letters to the architects' department suggesting improvements to the layout of school buildings, location of doors and windows etc to increase the efficiency of the building as a school and for more economical use of space.

Hot and cold

Age range
Seven to eleven.

Group size
Whole school working in classes or smaller groups.

What you need
Thermometers, note books, information leaflets and posters, electricity and fuel bills from the school.

What to do
The purpose of this activity is to make pupils aware of the need to conserve energy and to encourage them to suggest ways in which heating energy consumption can be reduced.

Approach your local authority to find out whether it has an energy management group from which you could

obtain posters and information leaflets. Make a display on energy consumption and ask the pupils what the message is. Ask the caretaker or headteacher to talk to the class about the way in which the school is heated.

Ask the children to make a list of various parts of the school where different temperature readings might be obtained. Let the children form small groups and, using a thermometer, record the temperature at a height of 0.5m above floor level (a single permanently fixed thermometer should be placed out of the sun on an internal wall 1.5m above the floor). The results can be represented in a table or a graph, or on a large plan of the school building if one is available. Let them identify hot spots and cold spots throughout the school. Explain that recommended temperatures are 18°C for classrooms, 14°C for corridors and gyms, and 21°C for medical rooms. Ask the pupils to conclude whether temperatures are too high or too low.

Follow-up
Ask the children to consider matters of heat loss, insulation, outside temperatures compared with inside, closed/open doors etc. Encourage them to suggest a school campaign to reduce energy consumption.

Continue their investigations into energy consumption with the following activity.

Light and dark

Age range
Seven to eleven.

Group size
Whole class organised in pairs.

What you need
Information leaflets on electricity consumption and maximum demand, note books, materials for producing displays.

What to do
This activity should follow on from the previous one on heating and can be part of work in science and mathematics.

Lighting accounts for the largest slice of electricity consumption, so use this as the basis of the activity. Begin by asking the children how many lights there are in the room. Why do we need electric lights? At which season of the year do we need them most? Why should we reduce energy consumption?

Ask the class to form pairs and conduct a survey of the number of lights in the school and, by means of their total wattage and the cost per unit of electricity, calculate how much it costs per hour, day, week, term and year to keep all the lights on.

Ask children during the survey to note any lights that are on for no good reason. Encourage pupils to suggest ways of reducing the consumption of electricity. For example, 'switching off' campaigns could be started and the caretaker could be asked if low energy bulbs and tubes could be used. Let the children calculate savings for the various suggestions they put forward.

Follow-up
Communicate the pupils' findings and recommendations to the governors (who will be grateful as the bills have to be paid from the school budget) and to the local energy efficiency officer, who might be persuaded to write a letter of congratulations.

Where we work 1

Age range
Five to seven.

Group size
Whole class.

What you need
Model-making materials (card, boxes, adhesive, paint etc), base board for model.

What to do
This activity leads pupils to consider their own working surroundings and how they might improve them. It will help them to locate their own 'place' in the classroom and to consider this in relation to their friends.

Begin by asking the children to think what their classroom would look like if it were smaller, then to try to make a scale model. Precise materials will depend on the nature of your classroom but the ideal would be approximately one metre square, with walls approximately 10cm high. Ask the pupils to make simple models of all the furniture and arrange them in their correct positions. Let them write their names on cards cut to fit the model of the table where they sit.

This is particularly useful in helping young children understand the nature of maps.

Follow-up
When the model is completed, encourage the children to suggest how the room might be rearranged. The layout of the actual classroom can then be reconsidered and attempts made to make it even more attractive in appearance by the addition of plants, pictures etc, as well as a determination to keep it tidy and litter free. Encourage the children to develop a healthy pride in their own surroundings which reflects a genuine concern for the environment.

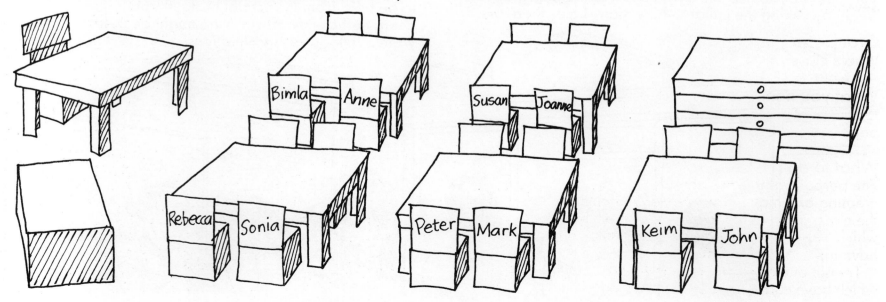

Where we work 2

Age range
Seven to eleven.

Group size
Whole class.

What you need
Writing materials, compasses, metre rules, drawing paper, pens, pencils.

What to do
The purpose of this activity is to involve pupils in creating and maintaining a pleasant environment within the classroom so that it becomes an enjoyable place in which to work. Ask them why they think it important to have a pleasant work place.

Try out one or more of the following activities, all of which have curricular applications:

● Ask the children to write a letter describing their classroom. They should mention the walls, the arrangement of the furniture, the view from the windows, and the direction in which the windows face etc (English).

● Let the pupils draw a map of the classroom having used a metre rule to measure dimensions. For older pupils the map can be drawn to scale. The arrangement of furniture can be as it is and/or as the pupils would like it to be (mathematics, geography).

● Encourage pupils to suggest ways in which they would like to improve the appearance of their room. First ask them to find out what is wrong with it. Are there any graffiti or dirty marks? Are there any litter or pieces of food left anywhere? Is the furniture arranged helpfully (are the waste bins in the right place; are there attractive displays of plants, flowers, objects etc)? Are animals kept in the right place and in appropriate cages, tanks etc? (art, technology, science).

- Ask the class to devise a 'green' display with posters and notices and a table where suitable objects can be displayed. Pupils should be encouraged to bring items for display (art, English).

Displays should be temporary and short lived, or frequently renewed to avoid the dusty dog-ear syndrome. Caring about the quality of the classroom environment should be a permanent and constant feature of class activity until it becomes normal acceptable behaviour. It needs to be as essential an ingredient of the classroom as is safety.

Who lives with us?

Age range
Five to eleven.

Group size
Whole class.

What you need
Hand lenses or maxispectors, specimen tubes, binoculars.

What to do
The purpose of this activity is to discover the range of animals living within the school building. Pupils will need to appreciate that some animals need our protection, some are of benefit to us, and others are not helpful to us. Some are friends and some are not.

Ask the children to observe where certain animals are to be found in school, for example, spiders, flies or ants.

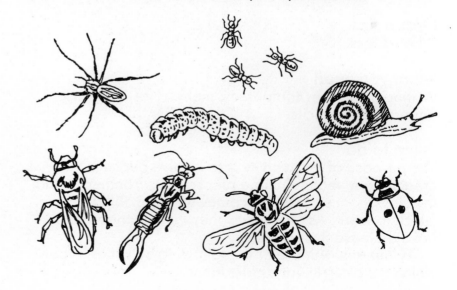

Animals which use the roof, such as birds and bats, may also be encouraged through the use of bird and bat boxes. Some smaller creatures can be captured and placed in specimen tubes for observation. Always remember to return them to their normal habitats. Any wild animals that have strayed from their natural habitat should be returned as soon as possible. Encourage the children to make a note of animal behaviour, their food, and, if possible, their lifecycle.

Some animals such as mice may well be found in schools and their presence regarded as undesirable if questions of hygiene are raised. You should consider humane ways of controlling mice through discussion with the pupils.

Bird behaviour can also be observed. In the autumn and winter encourage careful feeding of birds. Once a class has started to feed birds, however, they must continue to do so for the whole winter as certain species become dependent.

Follow-up
This activity can lead into curricular consideration of wildlife habitats and the interdependence of humans and other animals.

Materials

The key purpose of this section is to review the materials used in school, from paper for writing to the food served in the dining room. Initially, types and amounts of materials will be identified, looking especially at the raw materials from which items are made. An important point will be to consider the balance between natural and manufactured commodities. Activities suggested here are clearly linked with those in Chapters 4 and 5 which investigate waste and recycling in more detail.

While there are obvious curriculum links with science and technology in the activities suggested here, especially Science 6, Types and uses of materials, the main focus is on assessing what the school uses by way of materials in the context of a green approach to resources. It is more an information-gathering exercise, further designed to raise awareness of the link between what materials we use and the environment, and especially the need to be careful in our use of all materials.

All these activities are suitable for both rural and urban schools.

Chalk and talk

Age range
Seven to eleven.

Group size
Whole class, working in pairs.

What you need
Examples of all materials used during normal classroom activity (such as chalk, paper, adhesive), a selection of magazines from which pictures can be cut out, scissors, large sheets of display paper, notepads, pencils, felt-tipped pens.

What to do
The aim of this activity is to help pupils discover the source of all the materials that they use during lessons with a view to reducing the amount used and encouraging the use of alternatives wherever appropriate. This needs to be linked with recycling activities in Chapter 5.

Make a display of everyday materials used in the classroom and ask the children to work in pairs to list the items and suggest the raw materials used in their manufacture. When their lists are completed, organise a class discussion to agree an accurate list. Ask the children to make labels, either by cutting pictures out of magazines or by drawing, showing the sources of the classroom materials.

Encourage the children to suggest alternative sources, for example, using recycled paper wherever possible and restricting the amount of other material which might be wasted, for example, paint.

Follow-up
• Establish collections of suitable materials for use in craft work. Pupils should be encouraged to ask their parents to help.
• Arrange a reward for the most ingenious suggestion from a pupil for ways of economising on use of materials.

Where shall we put it?

Age range
Five to eleven.

Group size
Whole class.

What you need
A variety of storage containers.

What to do
Use this activity to support Levels 1, 2, 3 and 4 of Science 6. The aim is to develop ways of using a variety of containers to help keep the classroom tidy. With younger pupils, begin by showing them a range of containers in common classroom use and ask what they

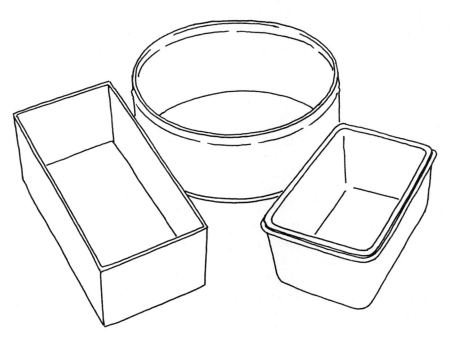

usually contain. Ask questions such as:
● What do we keep in them?
● Which is the biggest?
● Which is the smallest?
Compare their shape, colour and texture.
  Older pupils can discuss the materials from which the containers are made.
● What is the size and capacity of each container?
● What is the link between size and function of a container?
● What is the balance between natural and synthetic materials?
  Ask the children to suggest ways in which storage can be improved in the classroom. Always emphasise the need for sensible storage as part of a green approach.

Follow-up
Get the pupils to devise a range of labels to be used on all storage containers.

Wrap it up

Age range
Seven to eleven.

Group size
Whole class.

What you need
A number of miscellaneous items, some of which have been elaborately packaged using plastic and other materials, plastic carrier bags, paper bags, gift-wrapping paper.

What to do
The aim of this activity is to help pupils understand the reason for packaging and the need to avoid excessive packaging. Ask the school secretary to allow the class

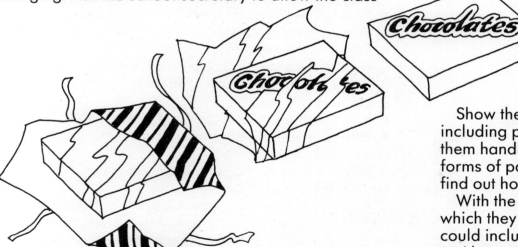

to open any packaged items which have arrived in school.

As a class draw up a list of items which pupils and their families may have bought, such as frozen fish fingers, potatoes, pairs of socks, a shirt, tights, baked beans etc. Ask the children to work in pairs and copy down the list, then beside each item write down the name of the appropriate form of packaging. Discuss with the class what they have written and what they have discovered about packaging.

Show the children various forms of packaging, including paper bags and plastic carrier bags and let them handle them. Ask them to write about the different forms of packaging, describing its various uses, and to find out how it is made.

With the class, devise a set of 'rules' for packaging which they can encourage their parents to follow. This could include the following:
● Always use bags and carriers more than once.
● Ask shops not to use too much packaging.

Let the children write to school suppliers and ask about their policy on packaging.

This activity should lead to some changes in practice. The curricular aspects are rather more limited than for some other activities, but this approach is consistent with the cross-curricular concern for the environment.

A splash of paint

Age range
Seven to eleven.

Group size
Whole class working individually.

What you need
Before embarking on this activity you need to research the school/authority policy on redecoration as certain types of paint or paper may be recommended. You will also need paint colour cards, samples of insulation materials, brochures on types of glass, flip chart or chalkboard.

What to do
This activity enables pupils to look more closely at the materials used in the fabric of the classroom, for example, its walls, curtains, blinds, windows, floors and ceiling. It will also aid understanding of design aspects of technology, in particular the suitability of materials for their purpose and the need for aesthetic considerations of colour and texture.

Ask pupils to suggest the range of materials used in building and decorating the classroom. These should include metal, wood, board, paint, screws, glass, fabric, flooring etc. Then ask the class to classify these according to various criteria such as:

- Made from natural materials;
- Synthetic;
- Warmth;
- Hardness.

Let the children add their own criteria to this list. Ask them to consider what properties we need from materials.

Let the children examine the various insulation materials, colour charts and brochures, then ask them to design a new classroom using a range of different materials. Encourage them to calculate the area of glass, board etc to be used and make decisions about degrees of insulation needed. Alternatively they can suggest ways in which the classroom can be improved by the use of different materials.

Let the children suggest a new colour scheme for the whole school and discuss its possible implementation at the next decoration period.

The impact of this activity will depend on how far reaching the school would like it to be. You may wish to introduce the idea of environment-friendly materials and how we should be seeking to use them.

Keep it clean

Age range
Nine to eleven.

Group size
Individuals to whole class.

What you need
Samples of all the cleaning and polishing materials used by the caretaker and cleaners, information leaflets from supermarkets about environment-friendly products.

What to do
This short activity is designed to alert pupils to the need for the use of 'green' products in the care of buildings. It can form, with some of the earlier activities in this chapter, a series of short, almost 'commercial-length', items, either as part of an assembly or as an introduction to some of the other activities. The ultimate aim is to ensure that the school uses only environment-friendly products.

Arrange a display of cleaning and polishing materials. Ask pupils to note down any captions on the containers indicating their 'green' properties. Some will have ozone-friendly aerosols, or contain products not tested on animals.

Ask the pupils to give the various products marks out of five for environment-friendliness. Older children might like to consider to what extent we can take manufacturers' claims at face value. Are products

necessarily as 'green' as they appear? For example, washing-up liquid has always been biodegradable, yet many now claim to have a new environment-friendly formula.

If necessary pupils can write to the purchasers of materials suggesting acceptable alternatives.

Follow-up
Get the children to calculate the capacity of various containers to estimate the amount used compared with the effects on shining floors and clean surfaces.

Food!

Age range
Five to eleven.

Group size
Whole school.

What you need
School menus, nutrition charts, leaflets from health education department, copies of photocopiable page 117, materials for making wall charts.

What to do
'Food!' will enable pupils to decide if the school diet is both healthy and friendly to the environment. Care should be taken not to offend particular religious groups as some have strict dietary rules and any hint that these practices are wrong would not be appreciated.

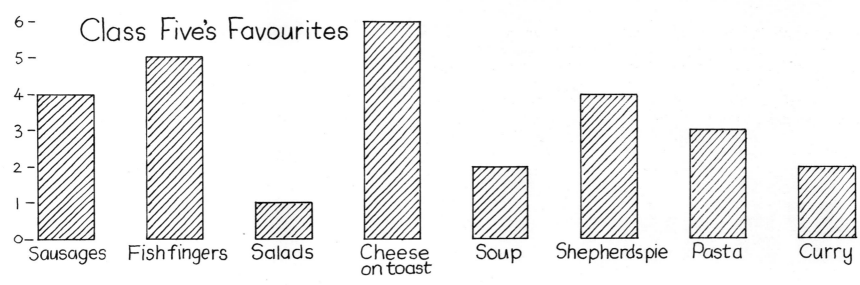

This activity needs to be considered in connection with Chapter 4.

Ask the children to use copies of page 117 or to devise their own questionnaires about school food. These should be adapted to the age range of the pupils, with younger ones being asked only what their favourite foods are. Let older pupils either keep a diary of what they eat for a week, or make a note of what they eat on one particular day. The questionnaire for older pupils can also include a list of their favourite foods.

Food consumption and certain types of foodstuffs have obvious 'green' connotations but care should be taken not to advocate a particular dietary view which might conflict with home influences. For example, while some people might feel that a clear case can be made out for certain types of diet on environmental grounds, it would be unwise for schools to deny choice to their pupils.

Ask the children to use evidence from the questionnaires to construct a number of charts and diagrams, ranging from a simple block diagram of preferences drawn by five- to seven-year-olds, to complex pie charts drawn by older pupils summarising the foods they have eaten over a given period. The latter would require classifying foods according to groups given on food and nutrition posters.

Ask the pupils to suggest ways in which school menus may be changed to a more balanced diet.

Introduce ideas about food production which can be linked to farm studies in both science and geography. Include reference to organic farming methods, particularly if the school grows vegetables.

Ask the school cook to talk to your class about the problems of catering and the difficulties of obtaining organically grown food.

Follow-up
The information gathered in this activity has considerable relevance to health education. While no studies in nutrition are required at this level for science, food studies are part of technology. Links can be developed here.

Waste

Waste and its disposal form a particularly important aspect of our concern for the environment which has an immediate appeal to parents and the local community. This owes much to the generally accepted link between waste and litter. The popular assumption is that litter represents a major mismanagement of waste, when in fact it is but a tiny, if visible, fraction.

It should be realised that the consideration of waste can bring with it feelings of guilt which may well hang heavy on young and sensitive minds. Your task is to encourage positive action to reduce the volume of waste produced, based on a valid policy for environmental conservation. The green school must set a correct balance of concern and action.

The topics covered in this and the following two chapters all feature in one of the science attainment targets, and the appropriate statements of attainment are worth repeating in full. Pupils should:

Science 5/1: Know that human activities produce a wide range of waste products.

Science 5/2a: Know that some waste products decay naturally but often do so over a long period of time.

Science 5/2b: Be able to keep a diary, in a variety of forms, of change over time.

Science 5/3b: Be able to give an account of a project to help improve the local environment.

Science 5/4: Know that some waste materials can be recycled.

Science 5/5a: Be able to describe the sources, implications and possible prevention of pollution.

Science 5/5b: Be able to classify waste products as biodegradable and non-biodegradable.

The question of responsibility needs to be considered in relation to the whole debate over waste and recycling. It also relates to a later series of activities in Chapter 6 on pollution. In the sense of being responsible for organising and working a system of waste management, the local authorities assume a number of roles. Waste management may also be the responsibility of a number of private companies, both to arrange waste collections under competitive tendering policies and to dispose of waste through privately managed sites.

At school level, both institutional and personal responsibility come into play. Each pupil is responsible for seeing that waste is properly dealt with, beginning with the elimination of litter. The school has a responsibility to see that waste is managed appropriately in all aspects of its operation: hence the involvement of cleaners and caretakers in the suggested school assembly.

Who likes litter?

Age range
Nine to eleven.

Group size
Whole class working in pairs.

What you need
Clipboards, paper, pens, materials for display.

What to do
The purpose of this activity is to familiarise pupils with the collection and processing of data, and to help them to appreciate the difference between waste and litter.

As a class, devise a series of questions to discover the attitudes of local people to litter and waste.

Some of the questions to include are:
- Where in our town/village is the most litter to be found?
- Who do you think are responsible for most of the litter: shopkeepers; shoppers; children; visitors; others?
- Who should be responsible for clearing litter: the local council; pedestrians; criminals on community service; dustbinmen; others?
- Would you be prepared to pay higher taxes or community charge for better control of litter?
- How far would you travel to use a domestic refuse site?
- Would you be prepared to put different sorts of waste into different bins?

Let the children work in pairs outside school, under adult supervision, to collect responses to these questions. Alternatively, encourage them to ask their parents and neighbours. Ask them to collate a summary table of results.

Follow-up
The survey results can be represented on a number of wall charts, using column or pie graphs to show the findings. The charts can be displayed in the classroom, in the entrance hall, or in the hall to be used during assembly. Ask the pupils to make comments on the results.

The waste gobbler

Age range
Five to nine.

Group size
Whole class.

What you need
A range of cardboard boxes, adhesive, tissue-paper, coloured paper, paints, clean litter.

What to do
The purpose of this activity is to make waste disposal a fun activity. Explain to the class that they are to design and make a large container in the shape of a monster to contain school or classroom waste. The monster will be called the waste gobbler and will need to be hollow with a big enough hole in the top to receive a range of dry waste.

Ask the children to design their waste gobblers on paper, then let the whole class vote for which one they are going to make. Encourage imaginative designs,

Our Waste Gobbler has eaten...

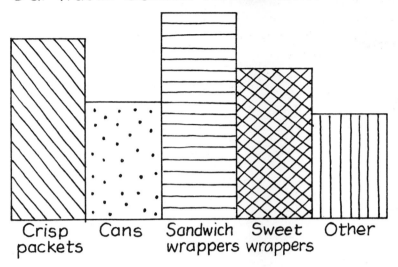

Crisp packets | Cans | Sandwich wrappers | Sweet wrappers | Other

using brightly coloured paper and plenty of clean litter stuck to the outside to make its purpose obvious. The monster can either be small and stand in the corner of the classroom, or large enough to collect litter from the whole school in the corridor or entrance hall.

Encourage the whole class to participate in building the waste gobbler and let the children devise and write captions to be stuck to the front of the monster encouraging others to use it.

Follow-up
When the monster is full, discuss with the caretaker or cleaners how best to empty it so as not to add further waste.

Each time it is emptied, let the children attempt some kind of analysis of its contents. How many different kinds of waste are there? How many different ways can they classify the waste? Encourage the use of various criteria such as colour, material, weight, size etc.

Water waste

Age range
Seven to eleven.

Group size
Whole class working in pairs.

What you need
Jugs, cylinders etc, for measuring volume of water, rulers, tape measures, stop watch, card, felt-tipped pens.

What to do
This is a class activity to determine how much water is used in a day. It may form part of a wider topic on water, which can also be linked to weather studies,

water shortage and the need to conserve this essential commodity. Pupils will also need to appreciate that water costs money and its misuse is wasteful in terms of money as well as resources. Introduce the activity with topical references to water, and in particular ask the children if they can estimate how much water we use in school.

Ask the children to form pairs to undertake the following tasks:
- Count the number of taps in the school.
- Find out how much water flows out of a tap in ten seconds and how much flows out in one minute.
- Measure the size of toilet cisterns. How much water is used when the toilet is flushed?

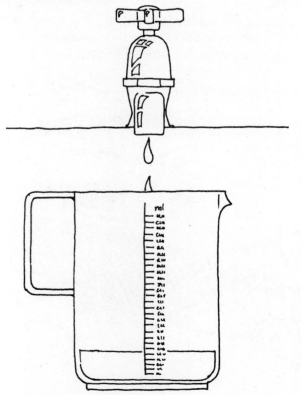

- If the tap drips, how long does it take to fill a litre jug?
- Make lists of the uses of water in school.
- Calculate how much water is used in school in a day, a week, a term and a year.
- Think of ways of saving water, for example not allowing the tap to run; reducing water in the toilet cisterns; using the washbasin plug and not allowing water to run away while washing hands, pots, brushes; not throwing water away if it can be used to water the garden plants.
- Design notices encouraging water saving and display them around the school.
- Link these 'green' activities to topics/curricular work on water.

Use the class findings and their recommendations in an assembly to encourage all pupils and teachers to save water. If the school has metered water, a careful check can be made on how successful the campaign has been.

Follow-up
As a class, test the quality of water available. Use a number of tests on tap water to discover whether it is hard, contains solids and, by taste and smell, whether any additives can be detected. Local water companies can usually supply leaflets on water quality. This information can be compared with the stated quality and ingredients of bottled water obtained in local shops.

Arrange a water tasting session using tap, boiled, filtered and bottled water and ask pupils to say which they prefer.

Paper waste

Age range
Seven to eleven.

Group size
Whole school.

What you need
Space to store paper.

What to do
Plan this activity well in advance, and perhaps use it as a lead-in to a recycling campaign. Involve all members of staff. Explain this activity as an investigation to find

out how much paper we waste. You may need to explain the term 'waste'. What do the children think it means?

Do not throw away any paper or card for a week. It will be necessary for all pupils and staff, including office staff, to co-operate. Some paper, for example, that which is greasy or dirty can be excluded from the collection. If possible, set a room aside!

At the end of the week let the pupils attempt to measure or weigh the paper just to see how much has been used. Ask the children to sort the paper and card into categories. For example:
- Writing;
- Drawing;
- Wrapping;
- Packaging;
- Printed;
- Plain.

What is the biggest category?

Paper and card used as part of pupil activities should be kept in drawers, folders and books, away from the collection, because this is not normally thrown away. Arrange a display of the waste paper collection in the hall or perhaps use it as part of the entrance hall display, with a large caption which reads 'This is how much paper we throw away in a week'.

Follow-up

Devise ways of reducing the waste. Pupils may have some ingenious, if not always practical, suggestions! Have a follow-up display to show the reduction in waste paper if a more efficient use of paper can be adopted.

There are many curricular applications for saving paper but it is important to consider links between trees and paper and between waste and litter (see references on page 127).

Food waste

Age range
Nine to eleven.

Group size
Whole class, working in small groups.

What you need
Tape-recorder, magazine pictures of food, scissors, mounting paper for collage, adhesive, copies of photocopiable page 118.

What to do
Wasting food is one of the more potentially disturbing aspects of waste as young people frequently link it with famine in the Third World. Care must be taken, therefore, to introduce this activity sensitively.

You may choose to take up only one of these suggestions. The approach to the school cook may also require tact, as discussion of waste may appear to be criticism of their professional competence.

● Arrange for two or three pupils to interview the school cook to find out how much food has to be ordered each week and how much waste has to be thrown away. Let them tape record the interview and play it back to the whole class.

● Ask each member of the class to say what their favourite food is. The answers can be represented as a

The co-operation of the school cook in any long term plan to 'green' the kitchen is essential. This is true not only for food, but also for all kitchen materials like soaps and detergents.

Curricular aspects of food and nutrition (science) or balanced diet (health education) and a concern for the conservation of world food resources (geography and environmental education) can be further developed.

Extend the surveys of food waste to the local food stores, supermarkets and street markets.

graph and the various types of food with their respective values can be indicated.

● Conduct a survey into the types of food the children eat each day for a week. They will need to come back after lunch and record what they have eaten that day and then to include how much they have wasted. A record chart is given on page 118. Alternatively, let the children devise their own.

Launch a campaign to reduce the amount of food wasted. Encourage pupils to eat a 'better' diet concentrating on reduced fat, more dietary fibre, more wholefoods. The use of posters, especially those drawn by pupils, will help. Use pictures of suitable foods from magazines to enable pupils to produce a collage of good food as part of the campaign for better and safer eating.

Throw away 1

Age range
Seven to eleven.

Group size
Whole class.

What you need
A collection of clean items that are normally thrown away (for example, yoghurt pots, bean tins, coke bottles, jam jars), packaged items (for example, box of cereal, box of sweets), pictures of commodities and packaged items from colour magazines, scissors, adhesive, sugar paper for collage.

What to do
This is an extension of, or an alternative approach to, 'Wrap it up' (see page 48). It needs to be part of a

larger programme concerned with the use of natural resources which may involve more than one activity from Chapter 3. There are obvious curricular applications in science and technology, especially in the introductory analysis of the items to be thrown away. Encourage pupils to see this as part of your school's green programme.

Provide the class with a range of items to be thrown away and ask them to arrange items in groups or sets using a range of criteria, for example, weight, size, colour, material etc. Ask pupils to write labels for each item describing what they are used for.

Bring one or two packaged items to school and let the children weigh them with their contents and again when the contents have been removed. Compare the weights of full and empty containers. Do we use more than we throw away?

Discuss with pupils why we need these kinds of packages and why it is necessary for them to be thrown away. For each item ask pupils to suggest alternative uses such as jam jars for vases, plastic bottles as cloches for plants. Use pictures from magazines to make a collage. Beside the collage ask the pupils to make two lists, one of the reusable goods and the other of the waste which needs to be thrown away.

Follow-up
Ask the children to keep a diary at home of all the items thrown away by their families for one week. At the end of the week, draw up a giant master list to demonstrate how much is actually thrown away by the families of the pupils in one class during one week.

Throw away 2

Age range
Five to seven.

Group size
Whole class.

What you need
Clean litter, items such as books and toys, paper sacks, large box labelled 'waste paper'.

What to do
Litter is commonly regarded as a major waste problem, when in fact it represents only a small fraction of what is disposed of in waste. Young children should nevertheless be encouraged to engage in practical activities of litter control. The intention here is to introduce the practice by means of a play activity.

Before the pupils arrive at school, scatter clean litter (for example, paper, washed drinks cans, bottles) all over the floor. Additionally, scatter some items which are obviously not litter, such as books and toys.

Observe the reaction of the pupils. Some may well start to pick things up and bring them to you. Ask them why they are doing this. They may say they want to clean up, or ask where they should put the 'valuable' items.

After a few minutes ask all the class to start picking up the litter and take it to the proper place. They may need to be directed to the waste paper box if they are unable to read the label.

When the room is tidy, discuss with them what they have done. What things are thrown away and what things should not be thrown away? What should we do with things to be thrown away? What different sorts of things are thrown away? Should they all be thrown into the same bin?

Follow-up

Ask children to design posters encouraging people not to drop litter. Children have designed excellent posters which are available from The Tidy Britain Group (see Resources, page 124).

This activity can be part of a whole school approach to waste collection and recycling. Bins and other receptacles can be placed in the classroom (and outside) for even the youngest pupils to use.

Encourage the children to talk about what is thrown away in the streets around their school.

Where does it go? 1

Age range
Nine to eleven.

Group size
Whole class.

What you need
The co-operation of the local authority waste collection and disposal officers, materials for model-making.

What to do
The purpose of this activity is to investigate local systems for the collection and disposal of waste. Information given to pupils should be carefully filtered as the issues are rather complex and experts tend to go into far more detail than it is possible for pupils to understand. Contact your local refuse collection/disposal officers with a view either to arrange a school visit to a suitable disposal site or to invite an official to talk to the children.

Most local authorities are anxious to encourage greater understanding, particularly among children. Suitable posters, leaflets, videos etc may be available.

Where does it go? 2

Age range
Nine to eleven.

Group size
Whole class.

What you need
Tape-recorder, note books, pencils, card, dressing-up clothes or suitable hats.

What to do
The purpose of this activity is for the class to prepare an assembly on the theme of waste disposal. Arrange for the children to interview teachers, cleaners, caretakers, dustbin men, local cleaning department officials or

This could lead to a whole topic on waste. Let the children make models of lorries, compacters, incinerators, land-fill sites etc using, among other things, waste items like cereal packets and other boxes.

Follow-up
This could be part of a whole school approach to dealing with waste. The investigations here could be used to provide the information on which the assembly drama in the following activity is based.

environmental health officers, then let them write a short play in which each of the characters explains his role in the disposal of waste items. For example, the teacher will explain how waste is put in the bin, the cleaner how bins are emptied, the caretaker how he collects waste from the cleaners and puts it in a large bin, the dustman how he collects it, and so on until the final stage is reached. This could be a land-fill site or an incinerator.

Develop the role-play for an assembly. Each pupil taking part should have a large card with a brief description of what she does. Conclude the assembly with statements about caring for the environment, of which waste management is one small part. Other readings, songs, prayers, can be chosen as appropriate to the school.

Follow-up
As with the previous activity, this could lead to a whole school approach to waste collection and recycling. The following activity can be used to illustrate what the children have discovered.

Where does our litter go?

Where does it go? 3

Age range
Seven to nine.

Group size
Whole class.

What you need
A range of waste materials, large sheets of sugar or other coloured paper, pins or staples.

What to do
Ask the class to make a collage showing the various stages of waste collection and disposal. It may be necessary to remind them of these stages from earlier activities.

The size of the collage will depend on the wall you wish to fill, but it could feature as part of a corridor entrance or assembly hall display. Build up the collage using appropriate pieces of waste material so that the medium is also the message! The information will obviously illustrate the actual local circumstances and may result from one or more of the other activities suggested here.

Follow-up
This will depend on the degree of accurate information obtained, and the location for the display. If sufficiently accurate, the collage can be drawn on to an A4 sheet and photocopied for adding notes or for colouring. They can be used as explanatory leaflets for visitors.

If the display is in a 'public' place, pupils may like to devise a short questionnaire about the information shown as a guide for other pupils in the school.

Recycling

Recycling would seem to offer a complete solution to the problem of waste and the whole concept of responsibility should underpin any scheme for recycling.

Recycling schemes frequently fail because the demand for recyclable material is not as great as is imagined and in some cases youthful enthusiasm becomes misdirected. The main difficulty arises because we tend to concentrate on the supply side of recycling, ie collecting paper, bottles etc, rather than the demand side, ie where it is to go and who is going to use it.

Early zeal in collecting newspapers was based on the assumption that it could all be recycled. The subsequent glut of soggy newsprint caused a price collapse and led to tonnes of waste, assiduously collected and baled as part of a school recycling scheme, ending up as land-fill.

The suggested activities in this chapter assume that you have investigated local arrangements. Many authorities now have staff available to advise on local recycling schemes, some have recycling hot-lines for easy access. Schools should give top priority to getting this kind of information before embarking on any scheme for recycling, be it paper, glass, plastic, cans, or anything else.

environmental advantages in disposing of waste glass in this way.

Recycling schemes are only worth starting if these become part of the ethos of the school. They are not short-term projects which lapse after a few weeks. For this reason they should not take up too much time initially and may well be introduced gradually.

Notes to parents should set out clearly the purpose and procedures for any recycling scheme. Initially attracted to the fundraising potential of such initiatives, some PTAs have found their source of income fluctuating wildly. An answer is to argue the advantages of recycling in the context of properly managed use of resources.

Clearly there is a demand for certain recyclable material. For example, good white waste, including computer print-out paper, is likely to be in reasonable demand and yield a good price, but its collection and delivery to paper mills is a matter of careful planning. Likewise, bottle banks may not be the full answer to the conservation of energy, given that the raw material of sand is hardly likely to be used up, but there are distinct

Curriculum applications are important. Appropriate attainment targets in science, technology and geography can draw upon examples and experience in recycling.

It is important for pupils to understand why it is a good idea to recycle materials. As far as paper is concerned, the raw material for paper production is soft wood such as spruce, which is not grown in tropical forests, but is farmed in Scandinavia and North America. It is a renewable resource. Pupils should nevertheless understand that often native broad-leafed trees are destroyed to develop these plantations and that the lack of light in these conifer forests makes it

difficult for ground cover plants to grow, thus destroying the habitat of various small animals. Using paper for recycling also saves energy because less is required using paper for pulp than using trees which have to be milled and crushed before pulping.

By contrast, cans, both aluminium and steel, depend on non-renewable metal ores. So if metal can be reclaimed as scrap, less ore needs to be mined from the ground. Reusing scrap metal also requires less energy, so saving cans for recycling has distinct advantages.

The whole question of recycling is a fascinating one, but clearly one with a high profile. The Government policy may well be a target of 50 per cent of recyclable waste to be recycled, but there is still a long way to go. Schools can play a significant part if teachers are aware of the complexity of issues involved.

Use it again 1

Age range
Five to eleven.

Group size
Whole school.

What you need
A number of labelled containers for each item to be recycled, materials for making posters, leaflets from the local recycling officer.

What to do
These activities must arise from a whole school policy on recycling. They should be preceded by careful planning and with the full co-operation of the appropriate authorities. Let the whole school become involved in the following activities.
● Write letters to the local recycling officer asking for details of local recycling schemes.

Use it again 2

Age group
Five to eleven.

Group size
Whole school.

What you need
Storage facilities, co-operative parents.

What to do
This activity should run in conjunction with the previous one. It is designed to encourage reuse rather than recycling or throwing away.

- Write letters to parents explaining the scheme.
- Design suitable posters to display around the school, with captions such as 'Don't Bin It – Recycle It'.
- Make attractive containers with suitable labels to receive materials.
- Sort the various items. For example, aluminium cans can be sorted from steel by the use of a magnet. Remember that both sorts are recyclable.
- Classes can be responsible on a rota basis for seeing that all materials are suitable for collection.
- In line with official instructions, materials for recycling can be dispatched. Remember, carrying very small loads by car will waste energy.
- All suitable waste (ie, not greasy or dirty) not being recycled should be compacted as much as possible before being placed in the waste bin.

Ask the children to suggest items in daily use which can be reused. The most obvious is drinks bottles which are returnable. These should be collected and returned at the instruction of the supplier. Other possible items for reuse can be paper bags; why only use them once? Plastic bags, jam jars, plastic containers of many kinds and food trays can all be reused.

Distinction must be drawn between those items which can be reused for their original purpose and those which can be reused for another purpose. The aim is to reduce waste by reuse. Teachers are highly skilled in using creatively what many would regard as waste. Pupils should therefore be encouraged to throw nothing away which can be reused, recycled, or used for craft etc.

Encourage the use of the following in the school's gardening projects:
- Plastic or other containers used as plant pots;
- Flowers and vegetables grown from seed using yoghurt pots;
- Plastic drinks bottles cut in half used as cloches.

Follow-up
The attitudes nurtured in school need to be extended to the daily activities of both teachers and pupils outside school. Give recognition to the best suggestions on reuse and recycling made by parents. Regular progress reports should be given in newsletters and Head's reports to encourage greater links between school and community.

Finding out

Age range
Nine to eleven.

Group size
Whole class working in groups of five or six.

What you need
Large scale maps of the local area, writing paper and envelopes.

What to do
The purpose of this activity is to find out by direct observation what facilities exist for recycling in the local area, where such facilities could be located, and to seek further information from official sources.

Before the activity, letters seeking information on recycling can be written, and sent in one envelope, to the local council. Then, begin the activity by outlining the purpose of the investigation and draw pupils' attention to aspects of safety when working outside the classroom. Arrange for supervised groups to investigate the neighbourhood and mark on the map any of the following: bottle banks, public refuse disposal sites, can

banks, skips for waste paper, and any other facility provided. If no provision at all is being made at present, ask the children to identify sites where such facilities could be located. Arrange for other groups to visit the local council offices and libraries to seek information on local recycling policies.

Field observation and recording promote geographical learning, and writing letters encourages English skills.

When the groups have completed their investigations, make a class display showing the local map with all the amenities marked. Copies of letters and replies can also be displayed, together with information obtained from the council offices.

The compost heap

Age range
Five to eleven.

Group size
Whole school.

What you need
A suitable undisturbed corner of the school grounds, chicken wire, wooden posts, hammer, nails, old carpet, an old wooden crate, small amount of organic manure, kitchen and garden waste, pencils, paper, thermometer.

What to do
This is a realistic form of recycling in which the whole school community can participate. Pupils need to understand that it is better to compost vegetable waste from the school kitchen and grounds than to burn it or throw it away. As this is a continuing process rather than

a single activity, it should be initiated, perhaps as part of an assembly or other whole school activity, and be referred to at times appropriate to the curriculum. For example, Science ATs 5/2a, 4 and 5b all refer to processes involved in making compost.

Help the children to design, construct and site the bin. A simple design is shown in Figure 1. This comprises a chicken wire basket supported by four posts, about one metre by one metre by one metre and lined with old carpet.

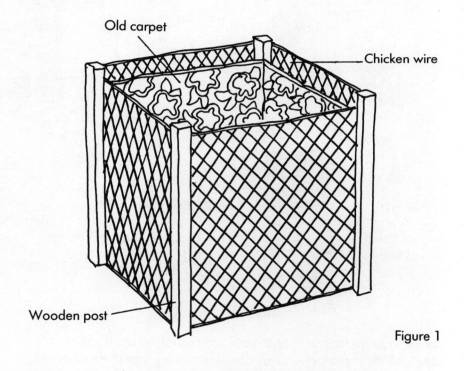

Old carpet

Chicken wire

Wooden post

Figure 1

A simple wooden box of similar dimensions with gaps between the side slats as in Figure 2 could also be used and may look neater. It should be placed straight on to level soil for ease of drainage.

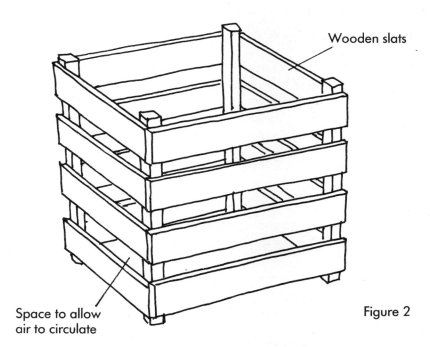

Wooden slats

Space to allow
air to circulate

Figure 2

Record the temperature at different depths in the compost heap, and at different times of year. Does this indicate anything about the speed of reaction within the heap? Temperature of the air outside the heap can be noted for comparison.

Follow-up
The produce from composting will be invaluable in the school garden. Alternatively, bags can be sold to parents to raise funds for other 'green' activities.

All vegetable matter, whether grass cuttings, cabbage leaves or weeds, can be used. A mixture of materials is best. Layers should be spread evenly across the bin with an occasional sprinkling of powdered organic manure to aid the reaction. Do not allow the heap to become too dry.

After six to twelve months the compost will be ready. It should be black or dark brown and of good texture.

Pupils need to be involved in all these activities and the co-operation of the school cook will ensure more rapid filling of the bin. Further advice will be found in most general gardening books.

If you have more than one compost bin, experiment with different types of waste to see which decays fastest. Records need to be kept of dates, amounts and types of waste put in each bin.

Make your own paper

Age range
Nine to eleven.

Group size
Three to four children.

What you need
Newspapers, mixing bowls, wooden spoons, water, paper moulds or old tights and a wooden frame, old sheets or towels, bottles, heavy weights.

What to do
This activity should form part of a series of lessons related to schemes for collecting paper for recycling. The result will not be as perfect as pupils might expect from the excellent quality of some recycled papers, but it will help them to understand the process.

Before the activity, obtain sufficient paper moulds for each group to have one. They can be bought from craft shops or made by stretching an old pair of tights across a simple wooden frame and nailing them in place as in Figure 1. Ask small groups of children to carry out the following process:
● Tear newspaper into small pieces and leave them to soak in water overnight in the mixing bowl.

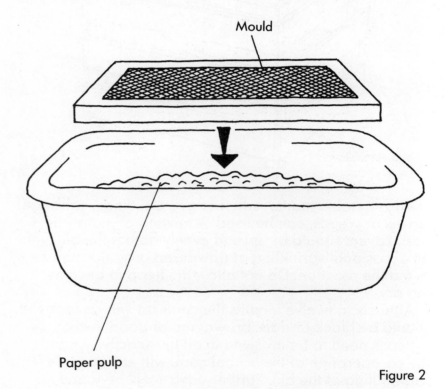

Mould

Paper pulp

Figure 2

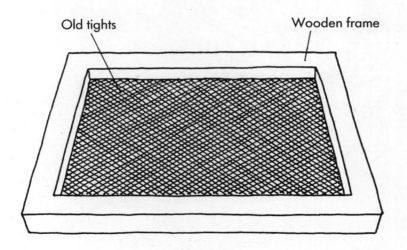

Old tights

Wooden frame

Figure 1

● Stir the mixture until it becomes a pulp, adding more water if necessary.
● Press the paper mould into the pulp until it is evenly covered (Figure 2).

- Lift the mould out of the pulp and allow any excess liquid to drain away.
- Place a towel over the mould, turn it upside down on to a table top and carefully press the pulp on to the towel (Figure 3).
- Remove the mould.

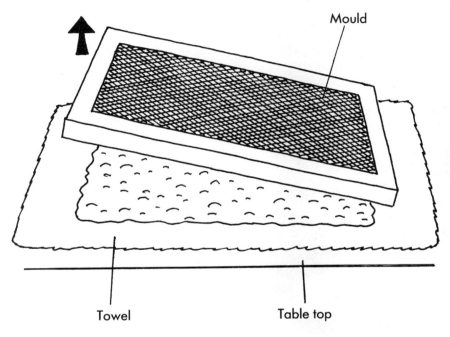

Figure 3

- Place another towel on top of the pulp and use a bottle to flatten it as in Figure 4.
- Place a heavy weight such as a large book on top of the pulp and leave it overnight.
- Remove the weight, peel away the towel and hang the paper up to dry.

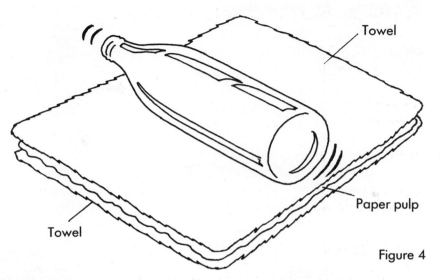

Figure 4

Follow-up

- Ask the children to suggest ways of improving this method of paper making and then experiment with them.
- Encourage them to suggest uses for the recycled paper. These could include collages or other craft activities.

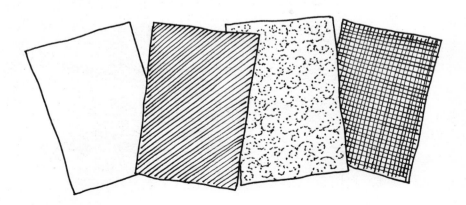

Bottle bankers

Age range
Five to seven.

Group size
Pairs.

What you need
Empty bottles of various sizes, shapes and colours, fabric scraps, knitting yarn, scrap paper, felt-tipped pens, fabric adhesive, writing paper, card, scissors.

What to do
The purpose of this activity is to introduce the concept of bottle banks to young children in an entertaining way. This should be part of a scheme to encourage pupils and their parents to use bottle banks.

Provide each pair with a bottle and a supply of fabric scraps, yarns and paper, and ask them to dress up the bottles to look like bank managers, bank clerks and bank customers.

Display the bottle puppets by arranging them on a table and making desks, counters and other bank furniture from card.

Ask the children to write balloon captions for the bank clerks and managers to tell their customers that they should use their bottle banks.

Follow-up
Involve older children by asking them to write short puppet plays to be used in assembly. The younger pupils can help with the performances.

Pollution

Levels of pollution sometimes cause distress to young people. They read or hear lurid press reports and begin to fear that they are surrounded with dangerous levels of pollution from which there is no escape.

The role of the school is to enable pupils to explore levels of pollution in their neighbourhood, to understand the degree of threat and urge appropriate action if something can be done about it.

Pupils should be encouraged to use the enquiry method of investigation to which they can contribute their own suggestions. This involves children in the initial identification of a problem, as well as being active participants in their own learning.

How clean is the air?

Age range
Five to eleven.

Group size
Whole class working individually or in pairs.

What you need
Pictures illustrating air pollution, note books and sketch pads, tissues, rain gauge, acid rain kit (available from WATCH, see Resources on page 124), pictures illustrating the effects of pollution, copies of photocopiable pages 119 and 120, magnifying glass or microscope, wind vane.

What to do
The purpose of this activity is to measure the level of air pollution around the school. How clean is the air around

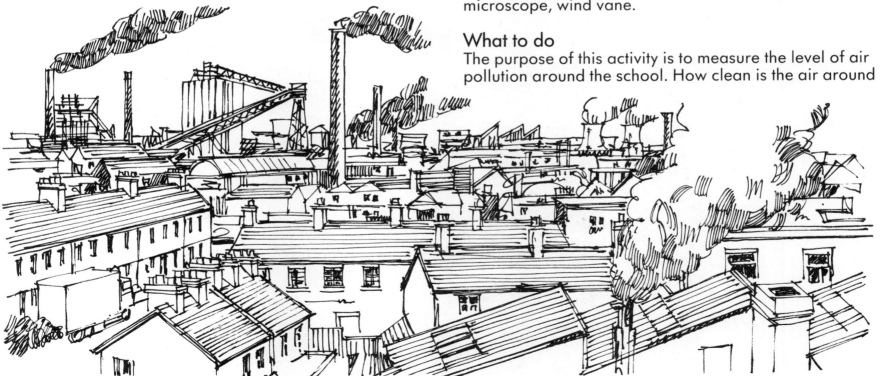

us? Present in the air are solids in the form of dust and smoke particles, liquids in the form of water vapour, and gases other than those which constitute the atmosphere.

Introduce the class to the concept of pollution, perhaps by displaying pictures which appear all too frequently in newspapers and magazines describing polluted environments. Be careful to use less dramatic examples with younger pupils. What do the children understand by the term 'pollution'? Can they think of any local examples?

Let the children undertake the following investigations:

• Use clean tissues to wipe the surface of leaves from broad-leaved evergreen trees like holly and laurel. What is found on the tissue and where did it come from? Is there a difference between newer leaves near the ends of branches and older leaves nearer the trunk? Can the children suggest other ways of detecting dust and dirt in the air? The 'dirt' can be studied under a magnifying glass or microscope. Tissues can also be mounted for display.

• Older pupils, aged nine to eleven, can investigate acid rain by using a kit available from WATCH (see Resources on page 124) or using universal indicator paper. Rain should be collected in a rain gauge and

tested as soon as possible. The acid rain investigation should be linked to the study of wind direction. Is there a link between wind direction and the degree of acidity? From where does the wind blow? Use a weather vane or anemometer to find out. Are there any large towns or heavy industrial sites situated in that direction? How far away are they? Children may be surprised at how far acid rain travels.

● Study the effect that pollution has on certain species of lichens. Some lichens are fairly resistant to pollution while others can only survive where the air is relatively clean. Lichens may be observed on school buildings, gravestones, trees, walls etc, according to the local environment. Ask the children to find and draw or describe the lichens growing near the school. Use photocopiable pages 119 and 120 to identify the lichens and assess the level of pollution in the area. This investigation may not be possible in heavily polluted areas.

These scientific investigations need to be recorded using graphs as far as possible.

Follow-up
Further observations can be made of the condition of building stone on churches and public buildings and on

gravestones. Limestone is generally more vulnerable to atmospheric acid.

Urban ideas
Air pollution is more likely in urban areas, although in some rural parts of the country industrial activity causes pollution to occur. Comparisons can be made between trees growing at different distances from main roads. To avoid danger from traffic you may need to collect leaves yourself and take them to school for analysis.

Pure water

Age range
Nine to eleven.

Group size
Pairs.

What you need
Jars for collecting water samples, measuring cylinders, shallow dishes, nets, copies of photocopiable pages 121 and 122.

What to do
Pupils may be concerned by reports of water pollution. Explain that water from rivers is not pure enough to drink but can be pure enough to support plant and animal life.

Obtain samples of water from local rivers, streams or ponds in jam jars. Label the jars with the source of water, allow the water to settle, then ask the pupils to describe what the water looks like. Check the jars at the beginning of the lesson and allow pupils to record the appearance every few minutes.

Alternatively, pour shaken water into shallow dishes and allow it to evaporate. Pupils can describe the residue and compare the results from different sources.

For field work activity, samples of river life should be obtained using a 'kick' sample. To do this, ask one child to kick the river bed gently while another stands downstream and traps in a net any small animals that are disturbed by the movements. Ask the pairs to take three samples in this way and put them in shallow dishes of river water for identification. The level of pollution can be measured by the presence or absence of certain fresh water invertebrates. An identification chart and results index are given on pages 121 and 122.

Caution
Health hazards exist in certain British rivers. Check with your local environmental education adviser before allowing children to wade into rivers. This activity will only be possible where there is reasonable access to a river.

Make sure that the children are closely supervised when carrying out these activities and obtain additional adult help if necessary.

What a noise!

Age range
Five to eleven.

Group size
Whole class.

What you need
Tape-recorders, sound amplifier, musical instruments (especially percussion).

What to do
Sound is important to us. Ask the children to name sounds with which they are familiar. Ask them to suggest

sounds we like to hear, those we prefer not to hear, and sounds which are useful such as doorbells or the noise of traffic when we are trying to cross the road.

Let them stand or sit quietly in the school grounds and write down all the sounds they hear, including birds, traffic, machinery, people etc. Let them write poems about the sounds they hear outside.

Introduce the idea that noise levels that are too high or too persistent represent a type of pollution. Inside the classroom, play sounds with increasing volume until they become uncomfortable and ask the children to raise their hands when the noise becomes too loud. This can be done with musical instruments as well as an amplifier.

Take the children outside to find and record examples of noise pollution. Suitable spots would include a footbridge across a motorway or the flight path of an airport.

Follow-up
Observations and recordings can be used as part of a topic on sound, including the speed of sound, and the importance of noise control. Encourage the pupils to make suggestions for reducing noise in the environment.

Unfriendly ozone

Age range
Seven to eleven.

Group size
Class to whole school.

What you need
Ozone pack from WATCH (see Resources, page 124).

What to do
The children will almost certainly have heard of the ozone layer which protects us from the harmful rays of the sun. However, at ground level ozone (O_3) is an indication of air pollution associated with car exhausts and high summer temperatures. Its presence can be detected by its effect on certain sensitive plants, especially a species of tobacco not easily obtained in Britain.

Fortunately WATCH is relaunching its Ozone Project during 1991 and a kit is available for primary schools to become involved in the investigation. It is probably unwise for a school to undertake an ozone survey in isolation so links with the national scheme are recommended.

(NOTE:) Reference is made in the Friends of the Earth Yearbook to the 'friendly' ozone layer 10 to 50km above the earth. If you undertake the Ozone Project you will need to underline for pupils that O_3 is helpful to us, in its proper place!

Rotting carriers

Age range
Seven to eleven.

Group size
Whole class.

What you need
A range of biodegradable and non-biodegradable items such as plastic bags (The Body Shop issues biodegradable plastic bags), newspaper, old woollen carpet, rubber sheeting etc, note books, pencils, scales, trowel.

What to do
One obvious cause of pollution is the amount of waste, particularly plastic, that is left lying around spoiling the environment. This activity will enable pupils to discover which materials are biodegradable and which ones are not.

Collect various unwanted items together and weigh them. Ask the children to list the items and record their

weight, together with a description of each. Make a note of the date.

Bury each item approximately half a metre deep in the school grounds, and mark the places carefully.

Dig the items up every two weeks and get the children ot observe and record their appearance and weight. Draw graphs of the findings.

Follow-up

This experiment can be used as the basis for a number of investigations on materials. At a suitable stage the partly decayed objects can be cleaned and mounted for an exhibition. Ask the pupils to write explanations of what has happened to each object.

Play on pollution

Age range
Nine to eleven.

Group size
Whole class, working in groups of five or six.

What you need
Dressing-up clothes, old curtain material, crêpe paper, card, paint.

What to do
This improvisation drama aims to help pupils identify causes of two types of pollution and to consider ways in which they can be prevented.

Ask the children to design and make symbolic costumes to represent pollutants such as sulphur

• Some friends go fishing by the river, only to find a number of dead dish, some killed by sludge. They also find swans killed by lead fishing weights.

Use the improvisations as a basis for an assembly and ask the class to explain to the audience in their own words how some of this pollution can be prevented.

Follow-up
Ask the class to write poems on the theme of their improvisations. Send a selection of poems to your local adviser or even to the local paper who may wish to publish them.

dioxide, soot, nitrates, sludge and tar. Devise a number of scenes on the subject of pollution which allow pupils to improvise. They can include:
• A group of children are playing on a beach. They swim in the sea and are covered with tar.
• A family goes shopping and meet cyclists wearing masks to protect them against air pollution. Tall chimneys deposit soot and discharge sulphur dioxide.

Campaigning

Concern for the environment is a key issue which links the school with the community. Public attention has in the past been drawn to environmental threats, and the need for remedial action, by a range of pressure groups, both local to international. Some, like the RSPB, have always achieved respectability, while others, like Greenpeace, have gained notoriety through spectacular and sometimes controversial direct action such as sailing into a nuclear test zone or coming between whales and their hunters. Consequently, campaigning may appear to be overtly political and outside the operation of primary schools. This conclusion would be unhelpful, denying pupils access to aspects of social education.

Within this chapter suggestions for activities are given that encourage consideration of what the school is trying to do in local, national and international contexts. Identifying local environmental needs, finding out about other organisations, developing concern for the global environment, are all activities in which pupils have a role to play, and can be a means to developing political awareness. This is not to say that schools should identify with individual political parties, but that pupils should be made aware of the political process and how individuals can take part in it through petitions, letters and debate.

Language features prominently in the National Curriculum as a cross-curricular skill, enabling pupils to develop competence in speaking, literacy and writing. These attributes form a substantial element in this chapter. Other means of communication like drama and display are also included.

Welcome to wildlife

Age range
Seven to eleven.

Group size
Whole class.

What you need
Maps of the school's wild area, card, paper, felt-tipped pens, materials for making marker posts for points of interest.

What to do
The aim of this activity is to publicise to parents the value and purpose of the school's wild area/nature reserve. Discuss with pupils why they should wish parents to know about the wild area and which aspects of it they would like to mention in particular.

Welcome to
Clifton
PrimarySchool
Wildlife
Experience

Encourage them to write a short trail guide in their own words, outlining the wildlife interest at each appropriate place on the trail. Maps and sketches of plants and animals likely to be seen can be included in the guide. Older pupils can act as editors and illustrators.

Let the children make large signs indicating directions to the wild area, plus numbered points of interest on the trail and posters with messages such as 'Don't miss our Nature Reserve' and 'Follow the Arrows to the Wildlife Experience'.

Follow-up
Encourage parents to contribute towards the maintenance of the wild area, either by making a donation or offering to undertake management tasks at the weekend or in the evening.

Urban ideas
Even if your school has very limited scope for a wild area, the suggestions under 'Coping with concrete' (see page 27) can provide a focus for parental interest.

Look local

Age range
Seven to eleven.

Group size
Whole class.

What you need
Cuttings from local newspapers highlighting local issues, letter writing materials and cards for names.

What to do
This activity depends entirely on local environmental issues. You first need to raise the pupils' awareness, either by discussing the issues with them, or arranging the news cuttings on a display board and asking for their comments.

Depending on the nature of the issue, try to develop awareness of what might be a suitable 'campaign'. If, for example, it is a new 'pedestrians only' part of town, you may wish to organise a simple simulation. Distribute cards to volunteers giving the roles they should play, such as shoppers, shop-keepers, residents, drivers etc. Each character should say what he thinks of the new traffic-free street. Ask the rest of the class to consider the various arguments which have been put forward. Can they agree on what would be the best course of action?

Encourage pupils to express their views in letters to the appropriate authority. Other ways of campaigning may be to draw up a petition to encourage parents to write letters, to organise a peaceful demonstration or to speak to governors. All these courses of action are particularly relevant in cases where decisions are being made which will affect the life of the school. For example, if a local nature reserve is being sold off for building land, the school will wish to make its views known, perhaps on behalf of governors, staff, parents and pupils.

It is important for the children to know the result of their action and for any replies from officials to be read to them, perhaps in assembly, and displayed on a notice-board for all to read. If appropriate, an official may be invited to visit the school to talk to the pupils, and respond to questions.

Saving the world

Age range
Five to eleven.

Group size
Whole class to whole school.

What you need
Information from outside organisations of global campaigns, such as threatened species, rainforest destruction, acid rain etc.

What to do
Pupils' involvement with local or even national environmental issues can give them a reference point to global concerns. You will need to select carefully from

the activities you undertake as part of the green school approach. For example:
● The issue of threatened species could involve on a local scale the protection of frogs and toads, both of which are endangered species. This could entail establishing and maintaining a pond and would need commitment and patience from the children in order to yield results. On a global scale, the children could consider the same issue by looking at the plight of marine mammals such as dolphins and whales.
● The issue of loss of trees could be addressed by the children on a local scale by planting suitable native trees. They should understand that the value of trees relates both to the wealth of wildlife dependent upon them (for example, the oak tree provides a home for nearly 300 different species) and to their part in maintaining oxygen levels and reducing carbon dioxide.

On a larger scale, the children could become involved in campaigning against the destruction of tropical rainforests.

● Pollution could be studied locally by testing rainwater and by looking at the visible effects of acid rain on vegetation and limestone in buildings. The effects of acid rain could also be looked at globally.

These global aspects each require secondary source material from pupils. References are frequently given in magazines and other publications. Encourage pupils to bring these in and incorporate them in wall displays.

Details and information are also available from organisations like WWF and FoE. Acid Rain packs are available from WATCH.

These activities can encourage pupils to contribute to national/international campaigns run by outside organisations. Their educational value would include linking the green approach of your school to the wider environmental movement, thus showing pupils that they are part of a much bigger group of people.

Money

Age range
Five to eleven.

Group size
Whole school, working initially in classes or smaller groups.

What you need
Promotional materials, a pupils' 'committee', links with the PTA, voting papers.

What to do
Schools need to raise funds for a whole variety of purposes. Money raised strictly for green issues needs to be set in the context of the entire PTA programme.

Involve pupils from the start in suggesting ways of raising money. Discuss with them the priorities, not only for items needed in school grounds and classrooms, such as pond liners and thermometers, but also for local and national charities concerned with the environment.

Each class should decide on a list of priorities, either through a committee to which suggestions are made by the class, or through the whole class. Older pupils may select priority items by means of a ballot of all class members, each pupil voting for their three favoured items. A final class list can then be submitted to a whole school committee and an agreed list sent to the PTA for their consideration. An alternative approach would be for each class to be responsible for its own fundraising, but this is likely to yield less than if the whole school campaign were backed by the PTA.

Items for which funds are required could include:

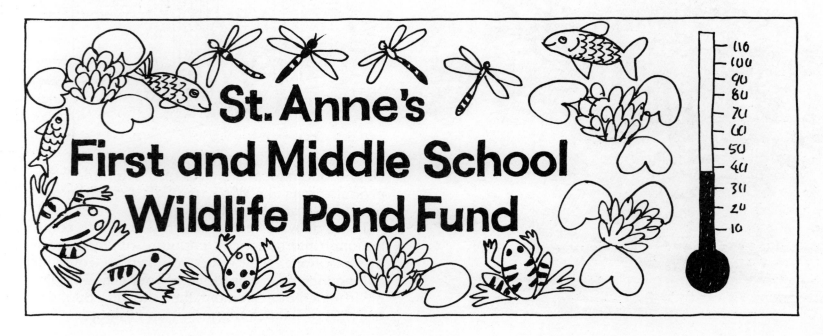

- International campaigns (Save the whale etc);
- Local nature reserves;
- Friends of the Earth school membership;
- Birdtables;
- Bat and bird boxes, or materials to make them;
- Pre-formed, or butyl, pond liners;
- Seeds, plants and trees;
- Greenhouse;
- Tools for gardening.

Suggestions for raising funds:
- Sponsored events;
- Odd jobs in neighbours' gardens (older pupils);
- Writing for sponsorship to local firms;
- Sales events using environment-friendly items;
- Donations for visits to the wild area;
- Stalls at annual fêtes;
- Recycling schemes, especially using cans and good white paper;
- Appeals.

Follow-up

Separate accounts should be kept of funds raised for green initiatives and a suitable indicator displayed in the entrance hall for visitors to see. As the total mounts, the list of items pinned next to the indicator, for which funds are requested, can be ticked off as the various targets are reached. This will encourage both pupils and the donors.

Urban ideas

It may be advisable to link fundraising more specifically to local projects in urban areas. Urban wildlife initiatives are less common than in rural environments so more encouragement may be required.

Join up

Age range
Five to eleven.

Group size
Whole school.

What you need
Details of relevant local and national organisations, including those to which pupils in schools can belong, materials for making badges.

What to do
The growing list of 'green' organisations may be confusing to pupils. The purpose here is to introduce them to a number of the better known groups, either as sources of information for their curriculum work, or as clubs and societies to which they can belong. Discuss with the pupils why it is helpful to belong to an organisation. Ask for suggestions, prompting replies that include learning more about the environment, attending events, receiving badges and magazines, and helping others as well as the environment.

Obtain information from both the local and national branches of organisations. The local wildlife trust is likely to have an education officer, or someone available to advise teachers and pupils. Pupils can write, with your guidance, asking for details of junior membership, sites to visit, suitable literature etc. Some authorities run clubs for primary pupils interested in the environment. If nothing exists, you might consider starting your own 'green' club as an out-of-school activity. Involve pupils in proposing ideas for membership, activities and designing badges. One school had a 'Green Gang' organised entirely by pupils interested in the environment.

National organisations may also have local groups. Obtain information from the following:
- Friends of the Earth;
- Greenpeace;
- Young Ornithologists Club (RSPB);
- WATCH (RSNC);
- WWF.

Encourage pupils to write as individuals for membership details. You will need to write for campaigning and educational material which you can incorporate in displays either in the classroom or in the entrance hall. You might consider school membership if there is enough interest generated in a specific organisation.

Use any materials received, such as leaflets or posters, to make a display. Devise simple quizzes and questionnaires for the children to encourage them to look closely at the display. Remember that it is important to maintain a balanced view of controversial issues.

Change the display frequently to avoid over-exposure, especially in the classroom where pupils have daily access to the material. If displays in the entrance hall are part of a half-termly exhibition organised by one class, topicality and relevance should be considered.

Urban ideas
Try to select material that is particularly relevant to the urban scene. Posters and displays should reflect aspects of urban wildlife and the quality of the built environment. Local urban study centres are useful sources for information, as is the Civic Trust (see Resources, page 124).

Local government links

Age range
Nine to eleven.

Group size
Whole class.

What you need
Copy of the local authority environmental charter, letter writing materials, paper and paint to make posters.

What to do
The purpose of this activity is to include pupils positively and helpfully in local government. As a result of growing interest in the environment, local government organisations such as the Association of County Councils are encouraging authorities to draft an environmental charter. Find out if your own authority has, or is planning to draft, such a document. If Green

Issues Committees or their equivalent exist in your local council they will no doubt be delighted to know that school pupils are interested in their deliberations.

Some of the terminology used in official documents may be too difficult for pupils so you may need to précis it for them.

Ask pupils if they can say who might be interested locally in helping the environment. Your local councillors may be prepared to talk to pupils and they will certainly be able to tell you about green issues. Again, pupils may be able to write to your representatives. It would be wise to include a covering letter. The purpose is to match your school's efforts against the aspirations of the local council. Pupils can read, or have read to them, the official document to determine how helpful it is. Pupils' comments may well be startling and not at all what council officials expect!

Some local authorities have their own campaigns to encourage, for example, energy conservation. Co-operation from schools would be welcome.

Pupils can design posters to draw the attention of visitors to the council's environment charter. Ask them to concentrate on just one or two aspects which they consider to be the most important.

Follow-up
Pupils may be able to monitor the progress of local authority initiatives on the environment if contact can be made either with a sympathetic councillor or with the council press officer.

Urban ideas
Green issues fall within the jurisdiction of metropolitan and other borough councils. You will need to investigate local circumstances at the town hall before embarking on this activity. It has great community potential!

Read all about it

Age range
Five to eleven.

Group size
Whole school working in small groups.

What you need
Reprographic facilities, computer or word-processor (optional), video camera.

What to do
This activity is aimed at publicising the school's 'green' activities. The method employed will depend on the facilities available in your school and guided suggestions made by the pupils.

Begin with a discussion of the influence of the media, especially television and newspapers. Younger pupils

will be more familiar with television and will perceive it in terms of entertainment rather than information. They need not be involved in early planning stages as they will find it difficult to appreciate what is required. They can be involved later on with interviews and illustrations.

For the primary school, two areas of media are most appropriate:

● Video: a simple camera may be borrowed or hired. Groups of pupils can be responsible for the story-board (script), camera, interviewing, captions etc. Without sophisticated editing equipment, results will be modest, but if tasks are undertaken by children a certain lack of polish will be understood. Shots can be taken of displays, pupils' work, a tour of the building and grounds, and the film can include interviews with the Head and other teachers, as well as parents, caretaker, cook etc, as appropriate to the range of activities undertaken. If editing is not possible, the 'shooting schedule' must be carefully controlled.

● Newspaper: it may be possible to obtain local sponsorship for a 'real' newspaper, but more likely is a photocopied product using school or teachers' centre facilities. Again, there are many opportunities for children to undertake a range of tasks such as reporters, illustrators, writers, editors, printers, distributors etc. It may be possible to link this with a mini-enterprise and cover costs by selling the paper. Parents can be asked to subscribe and copies can be put on sale to visitors.

Opportunities are afforded here for whole school involvement even if certain tasks are restricted to smaller groups. All pupils can be asked to make suggestions for content and to write or draw contributions.

Follow-up

If successful, newspapers can be issued at regular intervals to keep local people informed. It can be a medium for school campaigns and for publicising PTA activities. While the emphasis is on a green magazine approach, other school activities can be included. The opportunities for National Curriculum work, especially in English and technology, are particularly obvious in these activities.

Reproducible material

Planting trees and hedges, see page 21

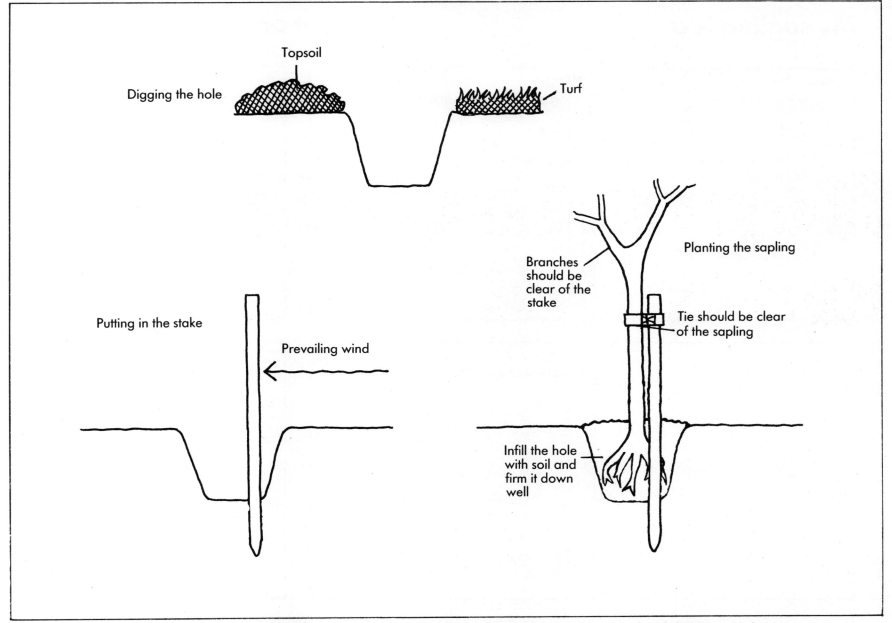

Digging the hole

Topsoil

Turf

Putting in the stake

Prevailing wind

Planting the sapling

Branches should be clear of the stake

Tie should be clear of the sapling

Infill the hole with soil and firm it down well

Planting trees and hedges, see page 21

My sapling is a   I planted it on

Date:
My sapling looks like this

Date:
My sapling looks like this

Date:
My sapling looks like this

Date:
My sapling looks like this

Date:
My sapling looks like this

Date:
My sapling looks like this

The air around, see page 26

What is the weather like today? Colour in the right box for each day of the week. What kind of weather has been most common this week?

FRI							
THURS							
WED							
TUES							
MON							

The air around, see page 26

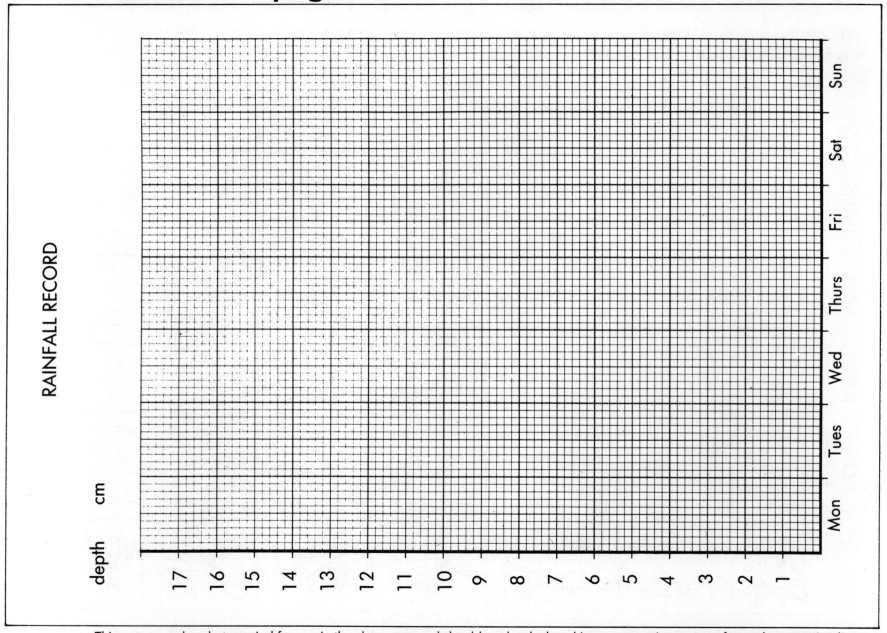

RAINFALL RECORD

depth cm

17 16 15 14 13 12 11 10 9 8 7 6 5 4 3 2 1

Mon Tues Wed Thurs Fri Sat Sun

Food! see page 52

SCHOOL DINNERS QUESTIONNAIRE

Do you like school food?

What is your favourite school meal?

What is your least favourite school meal?

What sort of food would you like to have at school?

What did you have for lunch today?

Do you know where the food comes from?

How do you think the food gets to your school?

Food waste, see page 63

FOOD SURVEY	Today I have eaten . . .	I wasted . . .
Mon		
Tues		
Wed		
Thurs		
Fri		

How clean is the air? see page 87

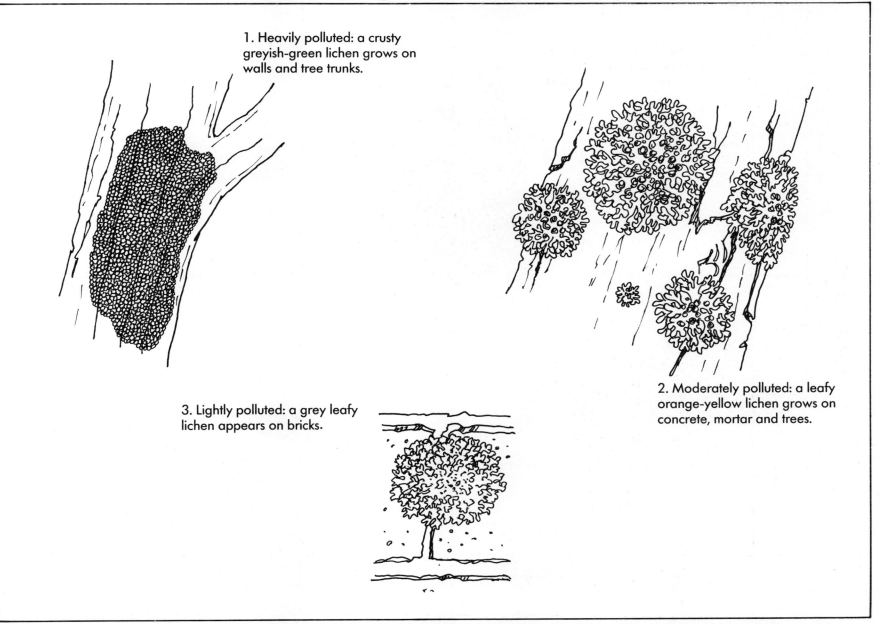

1. Heavily polluted: a crusty greyish-green lichen grows on walls and tree trunks.

2. Moderately polluted: a leafy orange-yellow lichen grows on concrete, mortar and trees.

3. Lightly polluted: a grey leafy lichen appears on bricks.

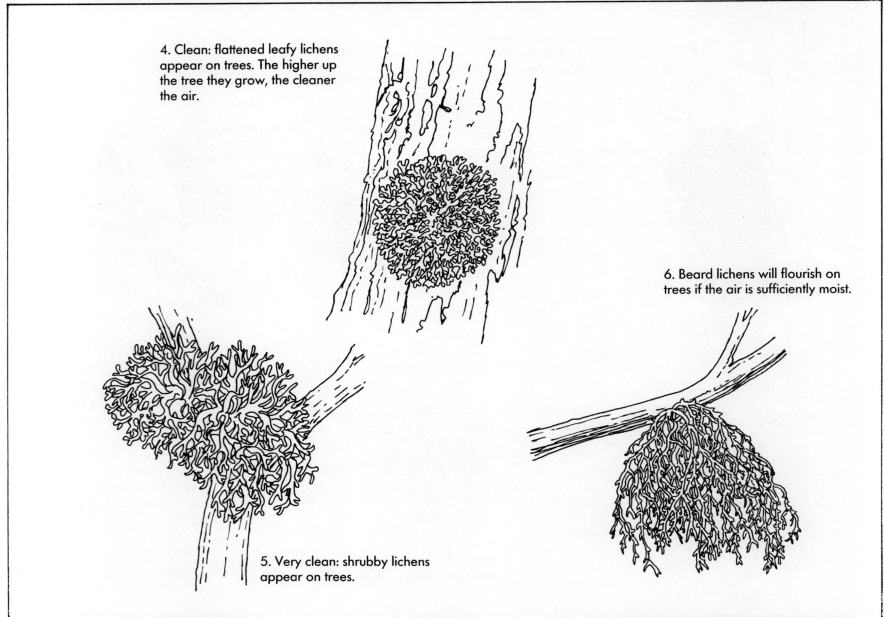

4. Clean: flattened leafy lichens appear on trees. The higher up the tree they grow, the cleaner the air.

6. Beard lichens will flourish on trees if the air is sufficiently moist.

5. Very clean: shrubby lichens appear on trees.

Caseless caddisfly larva
(up to 26mm)

Cased caddisfly larva
(up to 55mm)

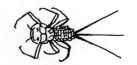

Flattened mayfly nymph
(up to 16mm)

Swimming mayfly nymph
(up to 11mm)

Freshwater shrimp
(up to 20mm)

Water louse
(up to 12mm)

Bloodworm
(up to 20mm)

Rat-tailed maggot
(up to 55mm including tube)

Pure water? see page 90

Less polluted   More polluted

An index of water purity

Tick if present

Mayfly nymph □

Caddisfly larva □

Freshwater shrimp □

Water louse □

Bloodworm □

Rat-tailed maggot □

Rotting carriers, see page 95

DECAY SURVEY										
Appearance										
Weight										
Object										
Date										

This page may be photocopied for use in the classroom and should not be declared in any return in respect of any photocopying licence.

Resources

Useful addresses

Centre for Alternative Technology,
Machynlleth,
Powys SY20 9AZ.

Civic Trust,
17 Carlton House Terrace,
London SW1Y 5AW.

Council for Environmental Education,
University of Reading,
London Road,
Reading RG1 5AQ.
(Schools can take out individual membership and
receive information on resources, etc.)

Friends of the Earth,
26-28 Underwood Street,
London N1 7JQ.
(A particularly valuable book from Friends of the Earth
is the Yearbook published in 1990 especially aimed at
young people. It contains a wealth of information and
practical ideas which teachers can adapt for classroom
use. Friends of the Earth also has its own Education
Officer and a school membership scheme.)

Greenpeace,
30-31 Islington Green,
London N1 8XE.
(Not much material available for pupils but Greenpeace
provides valuable campaign briefings, etc.)

Green Teacher,
Llys Awel,
22 Heol Pentrerhedyn,
Machynlleth,
Powys SY20 8DN.
(Green Teacher is a magazine published six times a year
for primary and secondary teachers. Also available
from Green Teacher is a useful book entitled Teaching
Green – a Parent's Guide to Education for Life on Earth.)

HMSO Publications Centre,
(mail & telephone orders only)
PO Box 276,
London SW8 5DT.
(Recent publications available include 'This Common
Inheritance: A summary of the White Paper on the
Environment'.)

Learning Through Landscapes,
3rd Floor,
Technology House,
Victoria Road,
Winchester,
Hants SO23 7DU.
(The Learning Through Landscapes Trust aims to
encourage widespread improvements to the
environmental quality and educational use of school
grounds.)

National Association for Environmental Education,
Wolverhampton Polytechnic,
Walsall Campus,
Gorway,
Walsall WS1 3BD.
(This is a professional association to which individuals
and schools may belong. Publishes termly journal
'Environmental Education'.)

National Association for Urban Studies,
The Canterbury Centre,
82 Alphege Lane,
Canterbury,
Kent CT1 2EB.
(Individuals and schools may join. Publishes 'Streetwise'

which emphasises urban environmental education.)

National Curriculum Council,
Albion Wharf,
25 Skeldergate,
York YO1 2XL.
(For official publications on the curriculum, including 'Curriculum Guidance 7: Environmental Education'.)

Nature Conservancy Council,
Northminster House,
Peterborough PE1 1UA.
(Some grant-aid is available for developing school grounds. Apply for details.)

Royal Society for Nature Conservation,
The Green,
Witham Park,
Waterside South,
Lincoln LN5 7JR.
(The RSNC will provide details of your local wildlife trust.)

Royal Society for the Protection of Birds,
The Lodge,
Sandy,
Beds SG19 2DL.
(The RSPB has excellent material for schools. The Young Ornithologists Club is the junior branch. Write for membership details.)

Royal Society for the Prevention of Cruelty to Animals,
The Causeway,
Horsham,
West Sussex RH12 1HG.
(Publications include 'Small Mammals in Schools'.)

Tidy Britain Group,
The Pier,

Wigan WN3 4EX.
(A wide range of teaching material is available. Send for a catalogue.)

WATCH,
RSNC,
The Green,
Witham Park,
Waterside South,
Lincoln LN5 7JR.
(WATCH is the junior branch of the Royal Society for Nature Conservation. It has its own education service.)

Woodland Trust,
Autumn Park,
Grantham,
Lincs NG31 6II.
(Produces materials for schools.)

World Wide Fund for Nature (UK),
Panda House,
Weyside Park,
Godalming,
Surrey GU7 1XR.
(WWF UK provides an excellent service to schools. A catalogue of resources is available.)

Books

Finding Out . . . About Managing Waste, (Hobsons Publishing PLC). Aimed at secondary school pupils, but a useful source of information for primary teachers.

The Conservation Project Book, Hilary Thompson & Shirley Thompson (Hodder & Stoughton). A colourful book with more practical ideas.

The Weather Project Book, Francis Wilson (Hodder & Stoughton). Includes information on global warming and human influence on the weather.

Wildlife Garden Notebook, Chris Baines (Oxford Illustrated Press, Yeovil). Although intended for developing your back garden, there are some useful ideas for school grounds.

The Outdoor Classroom: Educational Use, Landscape Design and Management of School Grounds (DES 1990). This book gives detailed information on the use of school grounds for a wide range of curriculum subjects.

The Final Report, Eileen Adams (Learning Through Landscapes). A report on the use, design, management and development of school grounds.

Using School Grounds as an Educational Resource, Kirsty Young (Learning Through Landscapes). Contains case studies, wall chart and colour photographs.

Ecology in the National Curriculum: a Practical Guide to Using School Grounds, P. Rupert Booth (Learning Through Landscapes). A useful guide to fulfilling Science ATs 1 and 2 in the setting of the school grounds.

Butterflies: a Practical Guide to their Study in School Grounds via the National Curriculum, John Feltwell (Learning Through Landscapes). Activities and practical work concerning butterflies and the environment.

Pond Design Guide for Schools, (Hampshire Books).

Inside-Outside, Cherry Mares & Robert Stephenson (The Tidy Britain Group, 1988). Suggestions for improvements to buildings and grounds. Also available from the Tidy Britain Group is a small leaflet entitled 'Initial Guide to Tidiness for Schools'.

The NAEE publishes a number of books for teachers, including: *Using the School Greenhouse; An Aquarium in School; Using Maps 5-13; Incubators in the Classroom; Developing a School Nature Reserve; Creating and Maintaining a Garden for Attracting Butterflies; Using Invertebrates in the Classroom.*

Countryside Charts, Macmillan Education. Wallcharts for 8-11 year olds on birds, pondlife, trees and countryside in danger.

Acknowledgements

The author and publishers wish to thank John Howson, education officer for Friends of the Earth, for his help in the preparation of this manuscript. Thanks are also due to WATCH for the use of their ideas in 'How clean is the air?' (page 87) and 'Unfriendly ozone' (page 94).